be
happy
be
you :)

Published by Collins
An imprint of HarperCollins Publishers
Westerhill Road, Bishopbriggs,
Glasgow G64 2QT

www.harpercollins.co.uk

© HarperCollins Publishers 2019

Collins® is a registered trademark
of HarperCollins Publishers Ltd.

Images on pages 33, 34, 53, 70, 156 and 173
© Shutterstock.com

All other illustrations © Josephine Dellow
Text © Penny Alexander and Becky Goddard-Hill

The contents of this publication are believed
correct at the time of printing. Nevertheless
the publisher can accept no responsibility for
errors or omissions, changes in the detail given
or for any expense or loss thereby caused.
A catalogue record for this book is available
from the British Library.

9780008367565

Printed in Great Britain by Bell and Bain Ltd

10 9 8 7 6 5 4 3

Thanks to all the team at HarperCollins
for championing happiness, and special
thanks to Michelle I'Anson and Lauren
Murray for all their wonderful support,
hard work and enthusiasm for be happy be
you. Thank you Josephine Dellow for the
magical illustrations.

Becky - My teen years were full of
wonderful friends and they have been
around ever since. With love to Helen, Mel
and Naomi, who held my hands throughout
my teens and have never let go. And to
my band of brothers, Charlie, Dave, Mikey
and Sweeny, who have always had my back.
Thank you, lovely friends, you mean the
world to me.

Penny - Thanks to all those characters
who made my teenage years in Macc and
Hull so much fun. Thanks to my parents
for all their patience. Thank you to the
teenagers I taught and my own children
- you have taught me so much. To all
teenagers everywhere on the journey now,
be happy, be you.

#behappybeyou

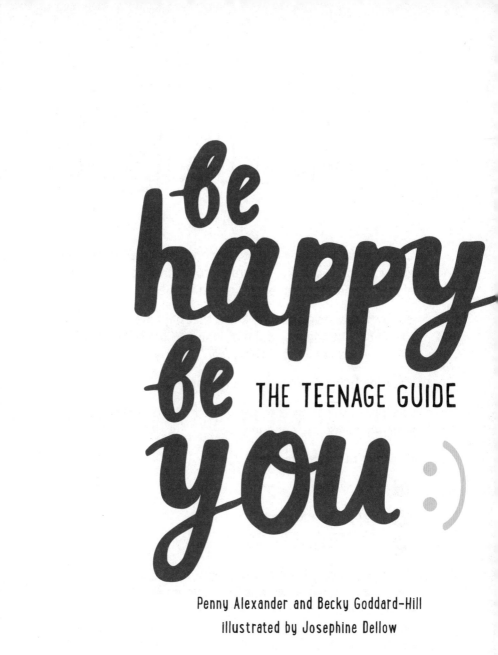

be happy be be you :)

THE TEENAGE GUIDE

Penny Alexander and Becky Goddard-Hill

illustrated by Josephine Dellow

HAPPINESS

Choosing to be happy is more important than anything else you do in your life. According to a survey, 72 percent of teens in Europe agree with this statement.

But even when you already know that happiness is down to choice, not chance, and that it should be top of your agenda, it can still prove tricky, can't it?

Knowing how to be happy can be hard.

The aim of this book is to show you how, to take control of your wellbeing and enhance it.

It is split into three sections:

 Happy You

 Happy Relationships

 Happy World

Teenage years can sometimes be turbulent, so each of the sections looks at various issues you might face, and includes actions you can take to make your life more positive and productive. Scientific research underpins each of the issues covered so you know why, not just how, each one works.

the teen years and your brain

MRI (magnetic resonance imaging) scanning has shown that our brains undergo massive structural changes during our teenage years. Important neural pathways are created that affect our future. This is a brilliant time to learn some happiness skills and take on board lots of ideas to help keep you emotionally well and strong.

The is the bit of our brain that deals with processing emotions like fear or pleasure. It is supersensitive and way more active during our teen years, and that's why you feel things very deeply. This can make the teen years tough. Learning a few ways to make yourself feel calmer and more positive is a very useful thing to do at this time.

destination: happiness

Do you ever think:

● If I only I was X I'd be happy.

● If only I did X I'd be happy.

● If only I was more like X I'd be happy.

If you do think like this (and we all do from time to time) then you are seeing happiness as a destination ... somewhere you need to arrive at.

In this book we are going to focus on happiness as being your journey, so you can enjoy your now, your everyday, not only when or if you get to X.

the hedonic treadmill

Truth is you don't need the right job, haircut, brand of trainer or group of friends in order to be happy, and even if you do get these things you are probably only happy for a little bit before you go back to feeling the way you did beforehand.

One study showed that even though they felt fantastic initially, lottery winners were no happier than non-winners eighteen months later.

Isn't that odd?

The same is true for those who have terrible, life-impacting accidents. Despite the initial trauma, people were generally found to return to their pre-accident levels of happiness – their baseline happiness level.

It is called the hedonic treadmill and means that no matter what happens, you will return again and again to your baseline happiness level, constantly looking for more happiness hits. It's exhausting.

A better option is to increase your baseline happiness, but is that even possible?

The answer is yes. And this book is going to show you how.

the magic 40 percent

Scientists reckon that 40 percent of your happiness is within your control, and that the rest is down to genetics and to circumstances. 40 percent, that's nearly half of all your happiness!

It's really worth focusing your energy on maxing out that 40 percent.

how to use this book

Think of this book like pick 'n' mix. Some of the activities will appeal to you hugely and will excite you and others may seem unappealing.

Repeat what works best for you,

but do try and give them all a go.

you will need

A notebook – there will be journal prompts throughout this book where we encourage you to write, draw and mind-map ideas. A diary is traditionally a record of events each day, whereas a journal is more fluid – you can try out different exercises, keep records, explore worries, hopes and fears, whatever you like.

There are no rights or wrongs, no rules. Some people find writing out the good and bad stuff helps, some people stick a timer on for 10 minutes and just write whatever needs to come out of their brain – a brain dump! Maybe your journal will be sketches and doodles rather than words?

Give it a try and find what feels good for you.

Happiness strategies are simple to learn and yet so powerful. You absolutely can be happy be you.

#behappybeyou

it starts with you

The only person you have by your side throughout your entire life to cheer you on every day and take care of your physical, social, spiritual and emotional wellbeing is... YOU!

So you need you to be in the best shape possible because you are your own caretaker and your own best friend.

me ↗

also me ←

you get to choose

Being happy is often down to choice, not chance, and almost half of your happiness is under your control.

How we look at things is all important and we urge you to see your ability to impact your own happiness as an amazing opportunity.

three types of happiness

Researchers have found that you can absolutely increase your happiness by designing your own life to include more pleasures, gratifications, and meaning. These are the three different types of happiness.

We are going to look at the different types of happiness throughout this chapter and show you how to weave more of them into the fabric of your beautifully designed life.

Simple pleasures are quick hits of happiness – things like eating chocolate, a first kiss, or feeling the sunshine on your face – and they give bursts of good feelings that up your mood. These feelings might not last long and you can grow used to them. That tenth bar of chocolate definitely won't taste as good as the first! But simple pleasures are speedy, effective ways to boost your mood.

Gratifications are activities that get us into a feeling of being 'in flow'. Unlike simple pleasures, the more you engage in gratifications, the more you enjoy them. Gratifications include things like meditation, learning to play guitar, or creating art.

Meaningful activities bring more long-lasting happiness. These could include activism, volunteering, or taking care of nature – all ways of making a difference to the world in some way.

So, let's do it. Let's make a start at increasing the happiness levels of the most important person you will ever take care of...

 You

(Then we will deal with the rest of the world and all the people in it!)

1 50 happy things

An attitude of gratitude brings great things.
Yogi Bhajan, Indian-American Sikh yogi

Focusing on the happy things in your life and giving thanks for them are two of the easiest ways to increase your happiness – simple, powerful actions that you can begin immediately to put into practice.

The things you focus on get bigger in your mind. So the more we focus on and notice the positive things in our lives – the things we are grateful for – the bigger they get in our minds and the more we can savour them and prolong their impact.

the science bit

Gratitude causes an increase in dopamine production in our brains (the feel-good hormone). This triggers our brains to want more gratitude (anything that triggers dopamine makes your brain want you to do it again). Our brains then start looking for more things to be grateful for.

gratitude has benefits such as:

 Better sleep and lower levels of anxiety and depression.

 Better exercise patterns and a decrease in physical pain.

Higher levels of optimism, determination, attention, enthusiasm, and energy.

And we could go on ... studies have proved again and again that focusing on the positives in your life and being grateful for them is hugely helpful (and rather addictive).

designing a happy life

Paul Dolan wrote a book called *Happiness by Design* in which he suggests we should 'decide, design, do' when it comes to happiness. In other words:

1 Decide what brings you pleasure and purpose.

2 Design your life so it is filled with these things.

3 Do them.

Again, simple stuff, but what a difference it makes to take control of your own happiness.

create a happy list

We all have loads of things that make us happy in life, but it's sometimes easy to forget that when we're having a bad day. Your challenge is to find fifty things that you are grateful for.

Do it as you see or experience things that make you happy, or as you recall them. It may take days or it may take months, it doesn't matter at all. It's about you looking purposefully for what makes you happy. As you record each happy thing say thank you for it – acknowledge how happy it has made you. (You can either do this out loud or in your head, it has exactly the same impact.)

If you get stuck then consider your senses. What sights, smells and sounds make you happy? What do you like to taste or touch? Or which people, which movies, which books, which sports do you like?

You may want to display this when it's done (or even in progress) to remind you of all the positives in your life that you are thankful for.

be happy be you...

...by designing your life to contain more of the things on your list. If some of these things aren't easily accessible – like a sunny holiday or a former teacher – you can always access them in your memory. Memory is a powerful place to go and can give you warm and happy feelings whenever you choose.

2 a can-do attitude

Whether you think you can.
or you think you can't. you are right.
Henry Ford, industrialist

changing your mind-set

A positive mind-set is not all about bright-coloured clothes and belting out hits from *The Greatest Showman*. It is rather about focusing on what you can control and what you can do, rather than focusing on what you can't.

Life is often tough and despite wanting to be a positive thinker and to have a sunny and optimistic attitude, there will be times when you may well feel defeated and despairing. This is real life after all and stuff happens. We can't pretend these hard times away, and not every cloud has a silver lining.

What do you do then if you can't magic the blues away? Well, you need to have a good cry or shout, talk it over, or journal how you feel. Whichever way works for you, it will help to acknowledge and express your feelings.

BUT you don't want to stay in that place for too long. You have a life to lead.

You cannot always create the practical changes that you might want to but you can always change your mindset to one of positivity, optimism and growth. The ability to bounce back after a tough time is called resilience and it's not something you either have or don't have, it is definitely something you can develop. And it is hugely helpful your whole life through.

the science bit

Did you know that you can change the shape of your brain? Sounds like something from a science fiction movie, doesn't it? But it's not; it is in fact an absolutely amazing power we all possess.

Scientist Dr Norman Doidge discovered that brains have the ability to be physically altered as a result of our thinking. This is called neuroplasticity. It means that if you purposefully and repeatedly think positive thoughts you can rewire your brain and strengthen those brain areas that stimulate positive feelings. You will be both happier and more instinctively positive as a result.

So let's get practising that can-do attitude.

When things are really tough you need to deliberately focus your mind on what you **CAN** do. It is such a better use of your energy than focusing on what you can't, and it trains your brain in problem-solving and positivity.

A positive can-do attitude really helps you to be more resilient.

Here are some examples of this in action:

- If you have a hard exam coming up and you are stressed you can focus on creating a revision plan and studying for it rather than focusing on your fear of the exam.

- If you see your friend being picked on at school, rather than feel helpless you can listen to your friend's worries and you can talk to a trusted adult.

now can you come up with can-do responses to these situations?

/ You missed a few weeks of school because you were poorly and are struggling to keep up in class. You can...

/ Your best friend has massively got into singing with her band and you are feeling lonely. You can...

/ You want to audition for the school play but you are too nervous. You can...

be happy be you...

...by taking control of your thoughts with a can-do attitude.

3 emotions

Feelings are much like waves.
We can't stop them from coming
but we can choose which one to surf.
Jonatan Martensson, footballer

How many different emotions do you experience in a day?
How many are pleasant, how many unpleasant?

All emotions are natural responses – we all have them –
even if some can be difficult or unpleasant to experience.
It's useful to keep in mind that they do serve a purpose and
they can be useful information to let us know how we're
doing and what we need to change. It's only by being aware
of all our emotions that we can truly experience happiness,
since we can't pick and choose which emotions we have.

Being able to identify and name our feelings helps us
to have some control over which ones we let affect our
thoughts and our actions.

the science bit

Researchers from Harvard University and the University of Washington attempted to map the development of emotion differentiation – *the ability to know and accurately label different emotions in yourself.* People with high emotion differentiation, who are good at naming their emotions, tend to use better coping strategies in times of stress, whereas those with low emotion differentiation, those who can't untangle their emotions, might turn to negative alternatives to deal with tough emotions, like aggression or alcohol.

So, if you don't understand your feelings you are more likely to act in negative ways.

You might think that your ability to label your emotions would get better each year, but it actually takes a dip at the start of your teenage years. Researchers think this is because teenagers are suddenly experiencing lots of complex emotions at once. As your emotions get more tangled and murky, they become harder to manage.

surf the happier waves

Keeping a diary or a journal can be a brilliant way to help you differentiate between emotions and create a bit of distance from them too. By identifying our emotions and then observing them from a distance, we can stop our feelings from developing into negative thoughts and actions.

Try these prompts to stay focused on surfing the good emotional waves:

1. List all the emotions you felt today, circle the positive ones and write about one of them. Celebrate the wins!

- Three things that made me feel happy today...

- Five things that made me feel calm today...

- I felt proud of myself when...

- I really enjoyed...

- My family admire me for my...

- Five small successes I had today were...

- The highlight of my day was...

- My best attribute is...

- Three unique things about me are...

- I'm excited for...

Five things or people I feel thankful for are...

I am in my element when...

My biggest success this week was...

I feel best about myself when...

Things that made me laugh today were...

struggling with a difficult emotion?

Try these journal prompts to help you pinpoint it. The more you are aware of a difficult feeling, the quicker you can intervene to stop it taking over.

If this feeling was a colour, it would be...

If this feeling was weather, it would be...

If this feeling was a landscape, it would be...

If this feeling was music, it would sound like...

If this feeling was an object, it would be...

Do you find that different prompts work for different feelings?

be happy be you...

...by using your journal to unpick emotions. Try different things and find what works for you. Look for the positives, celebrate the good things, be grateful and by all means brain-dump negatives, but try not to get lost in them!

4 the quest for self-identity

> Be yourself.
> Everyone else is already taken.
> Oscar Wilde, poet

Your teenage years are a time of delving deep into discovering who you are. Oscar Wilde makes a great point, it's important to know yourself first and to stay true to your sense of values and your feelings about what is right and what is wrong.

Because, when we're drawn too far away from our identity by others, we start to experience stress. It's exhausting pretending to be someone we're not. Whether that's trying to keep up piano lessons you hate just to please your mum, or behaving in a certain way in order to fit in with a group at school.

Self-identity is your understanding of yourself, it is a collection of thoughts and beliefs about yourself. It can be made up of things like personality attributes, knowledge of your skills and abilities, your interests and hobbies, beliefs and values and awareness of your body and mind.

You've probably become more aware that it changes depending on who you are with. So you will behave differently on your own to when you are with friends, and with family to with your best friend.

That's normal, although it can feel tiring at times, like you are lots of different people. Exploring your self-identity, bringing all those different 'selves' together and finding an identity that you are comfortable with is a big part of being a teenager.

the science bit

Identity isn't fixed. It changes throughout our lives, but a study of thousands of Dutch teenagers showed that changes in identity in teen years can be quite sudden.

At first anyway.

The study consisted of personality tests conducted on teenagers each year for six or seven years. In their early teen years, boys showed dips in self-control and self-discipline and the girls showed greater emotional instability.

But... the data showed that the dips were temporary. In other words, the more positive traits they had as children dipped, and then reappeared in older teen years.

Other people impact positively and negatively on our self-identity. This is why it is important to allow ourselves to explore what really drives us rather than follow the crowd or try to be what we think parents or teachers think we should be. Just because you are good at something doesn't mean you should do it for a living! Although, always take time to tune in when people who care point out your strengths, positive traits and skills to you.

Change can be scary, especially if it is sudden. But you are still YOU. Hold tight, the good news is that underneath all the change, an even bigger and better version of you is waiting to emerge.

Another big part of your self-identity you may find yourself exploring or questioning is your sexual orientation and gender identity.

Sexual orientation is about who you're attracted to and want to have romantic relationships with. Sexual orientation includes gay, lesbian, straight, bisexual, and it's totally normal to be unsure or not to want to label it.

Gender identity isn't about who you're attracted to, but about who you are – male, female, transgender, non-binary and many more – and it's also totally okay to be unsure, confused or to resist labels.

explore your identity

It can be hard to be objective about ourselves, but here are some ways you can do that...

1 Write the words 'Who Am I?' in the middle or at the top of a page. Then write down twenty things as soon as they come into your head. JUST WRITE. Don't scrub anything out or worry if it's right or wrong. You could put a timer on for five minutes. We promise it will give you a push.

2 Create a collage that celebrates your identity. You might want to include hobbies, interests, strengths and weaknesses, personality traits, likes and dislikes, beliefs, values, hopes and fears, dreams and ambitions, sexuality, gender.

3 Draw two big circles, one inside the other. In the middle circle write the personal characteristics of yours that you value most and won't change. In the outside circle write the characteristics you think are less stable. Perhaps the ones you think friends and growing up might be changing.

Use your journal to write down your thoughts. What bits of your identity are most fixed, which do you think are changing and why?

be happy be you...

...by recognising that your self-identity is changing rapidly, and allowing yourself time to reflect on who you are by yourself.

5 feed your inner creative

You can't use up creativity. The more you use the more you have.

Maya Angelou, author and activist

Creativity is about growing, taking risks, breaking rules, making mistakes and having a heap of fun. It doesn't always mean being an incredible artist, dancer, musician or performer. Creative thinking is a 'muscle' we all use every day, and one we can develop.

Fear of failing can be a huge barrier to trying something new though, so creativity expert Elizabeth Gilbert suggests imagining your projects as road trips. Fear can come along in the car, but there is no way fear is allowed to drive.

the science bit

Have you ever lost track of time working on a creative project? Psychologist Mihaly Csikszentmihalyi suggested that we experience a state called flow when working on creative activities we love. This contributes to an upward spiral of positive emotions and psychological wellbeing.

creativity and you

Some people might enjoy working hard at one project, while those who crave novelty might try lots of new things. Some might prefer to work on their own, whereas others might like group activities.

Remember, creativity doesn't have to be perfect. In fact aiming for perfection can make you feel stressed.

Try to have times where you relax and don't worry about the outcome being perfect. Things that don't fall into place straight away can teach us more than things we get perfect first time.

 Write down five ways you like to be creative.

What's your creative personality?

When do you experience flow?

Has a creative project ever gone wrong?

mind mapping

Mind mapping is a brilliant way to mirror and tap into the layout of your brain. Lists tell us what we already know, but mind maps let us create new ideas.

1 Write your topic, worry, theme or question in the middle of a page.

2 Add words as they come to mind, imagining each of your ideas as tree branches.

3 Play word association or let your mind wander. Don't say no to anything!

4 At first your ideas might seem obvious, but soon you will come up with less obvious ideas.

5 As your ideas slow down, look for words that link – you might want to connect them up with lines.

MIND MAP EXAMPLE

Check dates + £

Comic con?

Kitty Cafe?

I.O. milks at

I.O.u bike adventure + picnic voucher

Experience?

Sweets for whiskers, eyes + nose?

flapjacks?

BIRTH PRES

Cat theme?

Cake

Chocolate

Vanilla

Sci fi theme?

Cat?

Card

Cheesecake

aliens

alien

avoca

Strawberries

doctor who?

raspberries

area 51

alien face?

take me to your leader

cat
picture

Cat mug?

cat pens

Cats

Avocado

avocado
in a mug

make avocado
on toast?

ner

Likes

crime - Sci fi - aliens?

notebook

writing
Stories

pens-pencils

book
of short
stories

book
about
writing

MY
amazing
STORIES

sci fi?

crime?

google
this!

to

n

mer?

be happy be you...

...by making time for a creative activity that suits your
personality, and isn't perfect! Notice when you catch
yourself in the flow.

6 anxiety tool kit

You can't always control what goes on outside. But you can always control what goes on inside.
Wayne Dyer, self-help author

Life definitely isn't something you can always direct. Three exams on one day, hormones going crazy, parents refusing to give you more independence? Ahh yes, life outside of you is not always under your control and it really helps to accept and acknowledge that (even if it is really irritating). What you can control is how you feel and how you react. Both those things are in your hands even if it doesn't feel like it right now. Let's take a look at anxiety. Feeling anxious is just horrible and can feel completely overwhelming. But you know what? There are a whole lot of things you can do to control anxiety so it doesn't control you.

the science bit

Researchers believe that brain changes during adolescence do make teenage brains more vulnerable to depression and anxiety. One in three young people may experience some form of anxiety by the age of 18 and might need extra help from their GP or other specialists to overcome it.

Research has also shown that how we handle things has a direct impact on how much anxiety we feel. So the more strategies you have in your toolbox to help you cope with worry and anxiety, the more resilient you will become. Change the way you deal with worry and you will quickly lower your anxiety levels.

where do you feel anxiety?

Psychologically, anxiety can make you feel worried, uneasy, affect your sleep, give you poor concentration, make you irritable or feel like you are on high alert all the time and struggling to relax. Anxiety can make you tearful or in need of reassurance from others.

Physically, anxiety can make your heart pound, make you feel sick, dizzy, short of breath or faint. It can give you headaches or make you break out in a sweat or feel like you have butterflies in your stomach.

Anxiety can feel horrible, but it is important to remember it is a temporary feeling – it comes like a wave, but it crashes and passes by. The sooner you find ways to deal with it the less likely it is to grow.

draw or label where or how YOU feel anxiety

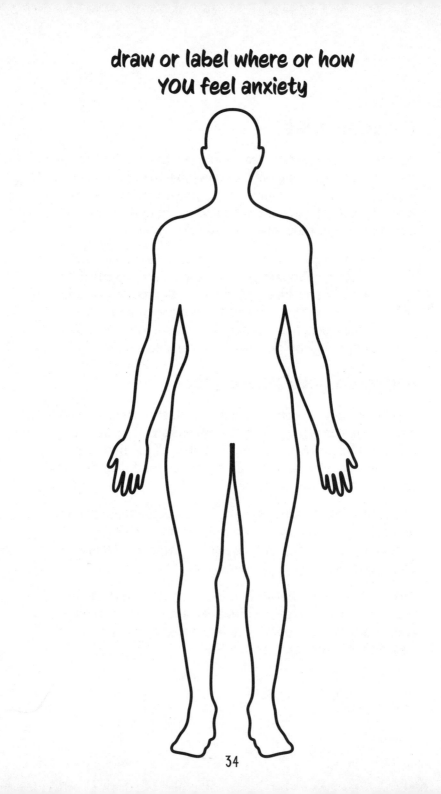

try some of these strategies to reduce anxiety:

⬡ Grounding yourself

Grounding yourself when you feel anxious works brilliantly. It is all about taking control and reminding yourself about what is real and where you are right now.

Why not try it ... first notice **five** things you can see, then **four** things you can touch, **three** things you can hear, **two** things you can smell and lastly **one** thing you can taste.

⬡ Breathing

Deep breathing and focusing on your breathing are actions that have been practised for thousands of years to calm the mind. When you are anxious your heart rate increases and your breath gets really shallow. Deep breathing helps get more oxygen into your bloodstream, which helps you calm down and lowers your stress levels.

Let's make it really easy to breathe deeply by using the power of your imagination. Find a comfortable upright sitting position and focus on your natural breathing.

Now imagine a feather in your hand. Take a deep breath in for a count of 4, then exhale slowly. Imagine blowing on the feather and it gently moving. Repeat the deep breaths in followed by gentle breaths out until you feel calmer.

Distraction

It's okay to distract yourself when you feel anxious; in fact it's a very good strategy. Figure out what works for you. It might be counting the beads on a chakra bracelet, rubbing a small stone or crystal you keep in your pocket, doing a maths problem in your head, or listening to some music you know will chill you out. Distracting your mind takes strength but as you do it again and again it will become a habit and a really useful one.

Mantra

A mantra is a motivational chant that is repeated to spur yourself on. It is often used in meditation to calm the mind. Mantras have been used for centuries to guide the mind's focus and are a brilliant tool for dealing with anxiety.

Neuroscientists have used advanced brain-imaging tools to show how mantras actually work, and they have found mantras help free a mind of background noise and calm your nervous system as a result.

'Ommm,' 'Peace' or 'My mind is clear and calm' could all work. Anything goes. You could choose a sound, a word or even a short phrase or prayer – as long as you repeat something with focused attention it will help you feel calmer

✎ When I am anxious I feel...

✎ It helps me to...

be happy be you...

...by recognising how and where anxiety affects you and trying out techniques to release it. There are lots more activities to help with this throughout the book.

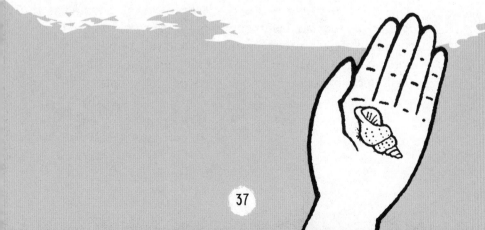

7 finding your happy place

Nobody can bring you peace but yourself.

Ralph Waldo Emerson, writer and philosopher

People often talk about their happy place. At the time of writing this there were over seven million images hashtagged #*happyplace* on Instagram – beaches, hills, living rooms, animals, gardens, sports, travel, hobbies.

the science bit

Researchers from Surrey University measured the brain activity of twenty volunteers as they were shown pictures of landscapes, houses, other locations and personally meaningful objects.

One thing they noticed was that the amygdala, that area of the brain associated with emotional responses, was fired up when shown places to which the individuals had strong personal ties. Favourite places stimulated a feeling of belonging, of being physically and emotionally safe.

go to a happier place

Your happy place doesn't have to be a place you can physically get to, because often we can't just leave the situation and location we are in. But you can *in your mind*, so it's worth having a happy place stored up for when you need to get away from stress, worry, anxiety or negative thoughts.

Set aside some quiet time to work on this. Get comfy, take some deep breaths...

Spend some time daydreaming about a place that makes you feel happy and secure. Work on all your senses until you can quickly bring it to mind and see, smell, hear, touch and even taste things in this place.

When you need some calm, perhaps at the start of a busy day, on the bus or walk to school, take a minute to remember your happy place.

/ Write a description of your happy place, or draw or stick a picture in your journal or somewhere you will see it each day.

How do you bring the calm of your happy place into everyday life? In real life, removing clutter and bringing elements of your happy place into your bedroom can all help.

Be happy be you...

...by using all your senses to conjure up a happy place.

8 weed out your worries

> Worry never robs tomorrow of its sorrow, it only saps today of its joy.
> Leo F. Buscaglia, author and lecturer

Sadly, worry is often wasted emotion. Humans spend a lot of time worrying about things that are highly unlikely to ever happen (zombie apocalypse), happen in a completely different way to the worry itself (you pass the exam) or actually turn out to be better than expected (you meet your new best mate at the party you were dreading going to).

Worries can also be your brain's way of telling you to act, so drawing up an action plan rather than letting worries take over is a great tactic. We will look at motivation in another chapter, which you might find helpful if you tend to worry about things that you need to get done. This section will show you how to weed out those negative thoughts.

the science bit

Thought challenging is a process in which we challenge the negative thinking patterns that make us feel worried, stressed or anxious and replace them with more positive, realistic thoughts.

This technique comes from Cognitive Behavioural Therapy (CBT for short), which might sound like something out of a sci-fi movie but is actually really about common sense.

Managing worry is all about *identifying your thoughts, challenging them and replacing negative thoughts with more realistic ones*. Imagine for a minute that your brain was a vegetable patch, thought challenging is weeding out the negative thoughts so the positive ones have more space to grow.

Sometimes worries can go round in circles, and become a downward spiral, which is why it's really important to have some simple tricks up your sleeve.

identify your worries

/ Write down the things that are causing anxiety in your journal. Just getting them out of your head can bring huge relief. Take a deep breath.

/ Congratulate yourself for facing up to your worries. Try and let the worries go for a while. Come back to your worries page a day later and ask yourself whether or not each worry is still an issue. If not, cross the worry out. If it's still relevant it's time for you to book in a worry session...

book in a worry session

Instead of letting worry take over, you can take control by scheduling a time to worry. Agree a time with an adult you trust, or a really good friend, and talk to them about what's worrying you, or else write out your worries.

Stick to a time limit of 10-20 minutes so it doesn't go on and on and get bigger and bigger. Focus first on emotions and then solutions – ending on solutions will absolutely make you feel more positive!

create your own worry tree

Can you use the worry tree to challenge a stubborn worry? The worry tree was included in the book *Managing Your Mind* by mental health and CBT experts, Butler and Hope, in 2007.

be happy be you...

...by reflecting on whether worries are worth your energy or not, by creating a space for problem-solving worry sessions, and by using strategies that allow you to let your worries go.

9 overcoming self-doubt

When I was younger. I just did it. I just acted. It was just there. So now when I receive recognition for my acting. I feel incredibly uncomfortable. I tend to turn in on myself. I feel like an imposter. It was just something I did.
Emma Watson, actress

I think the most creative people veer between ambition and anxiety, self-doubt and confidence. I definitely can relate to that. We all go through that: "Am I doing the right thing?" "Is this what I'm meant to be doing?"
Daniel Radcliffe, actor

Do you sometimes feel like you doubt yourself, even when you know you can do it or know you are good at something?

Perhaps when you are talking to somebody, you're worrying they're going to discover you're socially incompetent? Maybe you're giving a presentation at school and you're desperate to get it over with because you're convinced other people could do it better? Maybe it doesn't matter how many times you have done something, each time you start a new homework project, match, training session, music lesson, sketch or poem you worry you won't be good enough or that you will make a fool of yourself?

the science bit

Have you heard of imposter syndrome?

Someone with imposter syndrome doubts their accomplishments or their ability to do things and is afraid that they will be exposed as a fraud.

In the 1970s, psychologists Dr Pauline R. Clance and Dr Suzanne A. Imes studied 150 very successful women. Their colleagues thought they were impressive, they had won awards and scored highly in tests, but they all still put their success down to luck not skill.

Later research found that it wasn't just high-achieving women who feel like imposters, doubting our skills and worrying that people will uncover us as a fraud is a common human experience.

supporting yourself

Overcoming your self-doubt takes courage. But if you look back at your previous successes and experiences you can send self-doubt packing!

- Draw a table with four legs.

- On the top of the table write down the situation or task that is causing your self-doubt. It could be a social activity, school project, exam, Saturday job or hobby.

- Now, on each of the table legs write down one example of a time when you succeeded at something. It could be something similar. But, if you have never done this task or been in this situation before, think creatively of the skills you will need and think of other situations that might help.

- If you feel a pang of self-doubt, remember your strong table legs are holding you up, so your table absolutely can't wobble!

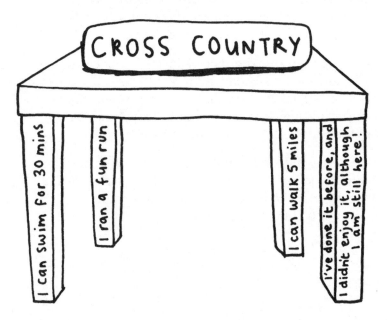

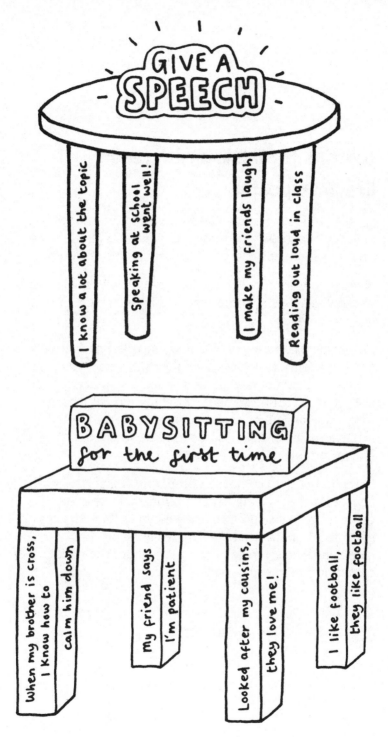

47

top tips for dealing with feeling like an imposter

Share your feelings, you'll be surprised to discover the majority of people have these feelings too. Even the lead actors in some of the highest-grossing films of all time.

Most people are too worried about their own self-doubts to notice yours! Spend some time people-watching and you will see it is true.

Help others. Focusing on encouraging other people who lack confidence in social situations can distract you from worrying about yourself because it lets you practise your skills. Can you bring someone else into a conversation who is keeping quiet, praise someone else for their achievements, or talk to someone else who looks uncomfortable?

Listen rather than compare. Comparing yourself to other people leads to finding faults in yourself. Instead of comparing, make sure you really listen to that person's story, think about what they are really saying, ask questions – how can you learn more about them instead of comparing yourself?

Limit social media when you feel wobbly. Worrying about what everyone else is doing can make a case of self-doubt much worse. Comparison is the thief of joy!

Have goals and stick to them.

When we feel like an imposter, it means we think our success is about being lucky rather than skilled.

We need to flip that...

Recognise and celebrate your achievements however big or small.

/ Set up a page in your journal where you list all your achievements. Keep adding to it.

be happy be you...

...by celebrating your achievements, building your table of confidence when faced with new challenges, helping others and avoiding comparison.

10 mindfulness

A day thinking about what could happen, should happen, or what might have been is a day missed.
Headspace.com

It may seem like a cool modern approach to being Zen, but actually mindfulness is an ancient art. Meditation (a form of mindfulness) has been around for thousands and thousands of years and a billion people have practised it, which suggests it's probably pretty useful, right?

Mindfulness is about being fully present and giving your attention to the now, not worrying about the past or future.

We need to be more firmly present in the moment so our mind can relax and we can feel clear headed. It is a great way to release stress and tension.

the science bit

Studies show that 50 percent of our waking time is spent with our mind wandering and this can cause us a great deal of angst. People who regularly practise mindfulness have been found to have lower levels of the stress hormone cortisol and greater focus.

We all need a little less stress and anxiety in our lives!

Mindfulness has also been shown in some studies to be on a par with antidepressants for treating mild to moderate symptoms of depression.

mindful word

The aim of this powerfully simple exercise is to give yourself mental space and help you be totally in the moment, allowing worries and fears to disappear and you to relax. Eyes open or closed, it is entirely up to you.

Come up with a word that makes you feel calm, a word like...

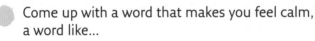

Sunshine   *Love*

Relax   *Breathe*

Think the word to yourself, say it slowly and repetitively in your mind. Say the word to yourself with each breath you take, in and out.

If you are on your own (or are entirely unselfconscious) say the word out loud between each breath cycle.

Keep your attention gently focused on your word. Just observe any bubbling thoughts and let them float away.

Do this every day for a week. Increase your time as you go. Once you have nailed this you can do it any time, anywhere you need to chill – on the bus, on the loo or even in class.

a quiet mind

Thoughts and feelings will float in whilst you are practising mindfulness. This is entirely natural. Try to just observe them – they are not you – and they will float away again.

Keeping a quiet mind can be really difficult at first and will require regular practice. But it is SO worth it. The goal is being able to be objective about your thoughts and feelings, rather than at the mercy of them.

be happy be you...

...by experimenting with lots of ways to practise mindfulness – walking, observation, visualisation, breathing exercises and so on. Try a few to see what works for you.

11 Body confidence

People still put beauty into a confining, narrow box. Think outside of the box. Pledge that you will look in the mirror and find the unique beauty in you.

Tyra Banks, model and entrepreneur

How we feel about our bodies can affect us hugely.

Poor body image can have a greater impact on your quality of life than you may realise – it can lead to eating disorders, social anxiety, depression and self-harm. Body confidence, on the other hand, makes us feel good.

the science bit

Research published in *Body Image* magazine discovered that:

- A woman's feelings about her body image are the third-strongest predictor of her happiness in life.

- A man's feelings about his appearance are the second-strongest predictor of his happiness.

Rightly or wrongly, in terms of our happiness, we need to get to a place where we feel good about our bodies.

change what you look at:

In one study participants were shown Instagram images of

 Celebrities

 Attractive peers

3 Travel destinations

Those who viewed the celebrity and peer images experienced a more negative mood and greater body dissatisfaction than those who viewed the travel images.

so what can we do?

Appearance-related social media usage can cause unhappiness, so try following social media accounts that share body confident messages. Watch TV shows and follow sports where all shapes and sizes of people are represented, such as wrestling, javelin, paralympics, gymnastics, shotput. Buy magazines that have things to say and which show diversity rather than ones that just focus on showing off clothes on models or body-shaming people.

Don't buy into a culture that makes you feel bad.

Changing where you look is very powerful.

media literacy

Research has shown that teens who are more thoughtful about their media use have better body confidence. You can use the FACE acronym when it comes to social media to help you feel in control of what you see.

Filter your accounts, removing those that make you feel insecure.

Avoid social media if it's making you unhappy.

Comparison is not healthy and often makes us feels dissatisfied, so focus on your own strengths instead.

Evaluate what you see. Lots and lots of images are fake, or designed to sell you something.

By being media-literate you can take back control.

body-confidence boosters

Every single person who ever lived is unique and interesting. Let's take a look at all the bits about you that make you happy. Look for the positives and you will find them. What do you like about you?

If you start to speak negatively to yourself about how you look, STOP immediately. Would you speak to your best friend like that? No, you'd fill their mind with positives and celebrate them. Treat yourself the same!

you're amazing

Next time you want to put your body down in some way, think instead about the absolutely amazing things it can do.

Try completing the sentences below.

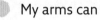 My arms can

My legs can

My hands can

My lips can

My hips can

My stomach can

My feet can

My eyes can

My ears can

How amazing is your body?

be happy be you...

...by appreciating that there is far more to your body than what it looks like.

12 mindful eating

When walking, walk. When eating, eat.
Zen proverb

Teen years are a time of rapid growth and change – you're probably being told that a lot now, right? Food and exercise are massively important. Your body is changing so fast that it needs extra nutrients.

Teenage years are also the time when you take over more responsibility for feeding your body and making choices about food. And that's on top of everything else you are juggling.

So it's not surprising, when you suddenly have all that choice and you are busy, that you sometimes opt for the less healthy options.

Teenagers don't have a great reputation for eating well. National survey data from the British Nutrition Foundation shows that, generally, teens' intakes of saturated fatty acids, salt and added sugars are all above recommended levels and that teenagers aren't getting enough of certain nutrients or enough exercise.

But dieting is just as unhealthy...

the science bit

Josie Spinardi has written about two really interesting studies. Firstly a review of every long-term diet study ever published by California University, which concluded that 'one of the best predictors of weight gain ... was having lost weight on a diet at some point.'

In the 1940s, there was a shortage of food after the Second World War, and scientists were asked to research safe levels for rations after the war. The study actually ended up discovering just how mentally unstable dieting makes humans. Incredibly, mentally and physically healthy men were given fewer calories than normally needed. They soon began to become utterly obsessed by food, buying cook books, thinking about food constantly and planning meals. Some chewed gum and binged when they secretly found food, some stole food and others became depressed and miserable. One even became obsessed with watching others eat.

Dieting doesn't sound mentally or physically healthy, does it?

The best ways to be healthy are simple:

 Eat a balanced diet.

 Eat mindfully.

a healthy balance

We are sure you know what a healthy plate looks like, you've probably had it drummed into you since you were at primary school. A healthy diet has balance, with treats in moderation.

Sadly, ice cream, crisps, cakes, chocolate and biscuits don't really bring nutritional value to the table, so the advice is to keep them as treats. That's much easier to do when you eat mindfully.

how to eat mindfully

Research suggests that healthy eating is mindful. It's about thinking through what food your body really needs, and eating to your hunger. Believe it or not human bodies do know how to do it naturally, but we need to really listen to our bodies to remember how to do this.

Start by picking one meal a day to try these tips on...

- Listen to your body's physical hunger cues. Eat when you are hungry and only until you are full.

- If you have a choice of what to eat, take some time to think about how the food you choose will make you feel, mentally and physically, not just as you eat it, but afterwards too.

Sit down to eat and stay there until you have finished, rather than wandering round or doing other things.

Use your senses – notice the colours, smells, sounds, textures and flavours of your food.

Eat without distractions like the TV or your phone.

Eat slowly, it takes twenty minutes for fullness signals to reach our brain!

Appreciate and be grateful for your food.

Notice how different foods make you feel, not just when you are eating, but afterwards.

Learn to distinguish between true hunger and feeling a need to eat for other reasons like stress or boredom.

Be aware of emotions getting tangled up in your food – guilt and anxiety about food create, rather than solve, problems.

Get involved in family meal-planning, learning to cook and making meals that really excite your senses!

Write a description of your favourite healthy meal using as many words to describe each of the senses as you can jam pack in. Come back to this when you need a reminder to eat healthily and happily.

be happy be you...

...by practising mindful eating strategies to stay focused on being healthy and happy around food.

13 how to be assertive

> The way we communicate with others and with ourselves ultimately determines the quality of our lives.
> Anthony Robbins, author and life coach

Being assertive is a skill that you will benefit from tremendously. We suggest you practise it until it becomes a habit (that's us being assertive).

You have to PRACTISE being assertive! Do it NOW or else!!!!! (oops – a bit aggressive).

Erm, perhaps you might want to possibly think about being assertive, if you would like to? (That's us being passive.)

the science bit

Research has shown that when we're less assertive, we experience more vulnerability and are more susceptible to depression. This is partly because we don't feel in control of what is happening to us.

If you are assertive you are saying loud and clear: I respect myself.

If you respect yourself it is MUCH more likely other people will respect you too. You will be happier because you are not being trodden on or doing the treading on (neither of which feels nice).

you can learn to be assertive

Passive people avoid eye contact, speak quietly and don't voice their opinions. They often get overlooked.

Aggressive people shout and demand that their needs are met. They are often disliked.

Assertive people are polite, they look confident and relaxed and state clearly what they want, think, feel or need. They use 'I' statements. They respect other people.

You don't need to be born with an assertive personality – it is a skill (like juggling) that you can learn.

so how does it help?

Being assertive can help you in brilliant ways like standing up for your rights. It can help you say what you want to happen, ask questions and access help. It can help you say no.

so, let's practise...

Pause and plan.

Before you react in any situation pause and plan your assertive response.

Try this...

Someone that you aren't interested in asks you if you want to go out on a date. Circle the assertive response:

1. No, thank you.

2. Get lost. Why would I want to go out with you?

3. I'm not really sure ... maybe, oh go on then, I suppose...

The assertive response (we know you got it right) is polite and clear. It avoids tricky situations and it avoids hurting someone's feelings more than necessary (they might hurt a bit just because you said no, but that's not your responsibility!).

Start being assertive about small things, such as asking your parents for a later bedtime. Practise with the small things till you feel strong and ready to tackle the big stuff. Often fear, doubt or guilt stops us, but by having a go we soon realise the roof doesn't fall in if we speak up.

Studying people secretly is great fun. Study assertive people who say how they feel and what they want respectfully. Take notes and copy their behaviour. The world around you is your best teacher.

be happy be you...

...by taking care of yourself and your needs all through your life, and practise being assertive until it becomes second nature.

14 getting good sleep

The amount of sleep required by the average person is five minutes more.
Wilson Mizner, playwright

So how are you sleeping these days?

Do you find it harder to get to sleep and much harder to get up? Do you get the word lazy thrown at you? In teen years sleep really does change (and it has nothing to do with laziness).

the science bit

At night, levels of the 'darkness hormone' melatonin increase, helping us to fall asleep. Most adults start to produce melatonin at about 10 p.m. A sleep lab study of teens discovered that they only began to produce the hormone at 1 a.m.

AHA!

It explains a lot, but what causes that melatonin difference?

sleep biology

Scientists have discovered sleep patterns change during the teen years because the brain's circadian system (biological clock) changes. The usual childhood pattern of 'getting up early and going to bed early' changes, to a 'go to bed late and get up late' pattern. Sadly parents and schools don't usually take this on board!

sleep behaviour

Often when teens stay up late they watch TV or play games on their phone/tablet. The bright lights could cause melatonin release to be delayed, making sleep even more difficult.

So, as well as biology it could also be behaviour that is stopping you from sleeping and that's brilliant, because that is something you can control.

A study in the *Journal of Sleep Research* showed teenagers need 9.5 hours' sleep a night, but on average only get 7.5 hours.

You might find you sleep in longer at the weekend to catch up on all your missed sleep. Sounds good in theory but this causes havoc with your sleep patterns, plus you lose half your weekend!

the impact of sleeping well

When you don't get enough sleep it affects so many areas of your life. It can:

- Affect your ability to learn and problem-solve.
- Make you bad tempered and impatient.
- Make you feel poorly.
- Make you feel depressed.

It can ruin everything.

And a recent life satisfaction study found that sleep quality was the single most influential factor in rating daily mood, too.

Sleeping well is one of the very best things you can do to make yourself happy, healthy, smart and good to be around.

how to get enough sleep

- A regular bedtime and wake-up time every day gets your body into a good pattern.

- Having a regular bedtime routine, e.g bath, book, glass of milk, will trigger your brain into knowing it's time to sleep.

- Avoid technology for an hour before you sleep and turn it all off/take it out of your room so the lights don't disturb you and you have no temptation.

- Aim for at least 60 minutes' exercise every day and lots of daylight.

- Avoid caffeine after 6 p.m.

- Listen to gentle music.

- Use guided meditations, talking things through, or journaling to empty a busy mind before you go to sleep.

bedtime routine

Devise a bedtime routine for yourself, including some of the actions above (and definitely including timings). Write it up on a card and place it somewhere you can see it and don't forget, follow this to the letter for a week and then reflect on how it has worked for you.

be happy be you...

...by taking responsibility for getting enough sleep so that you feel your best self.

15 smashing your goals

> A goal without a plan is just a wish.
> **Antoine de Saint-Exupéry, author**

It is hugely important to enjoy the journey of life, but achieving your goals can be fabulous too. Goals help us focus our behaviour and help us achieve our dreams.

Your goals will be as individual as you are. You may aspire to climb a mountain, get good grades, make more friends, eat more healthily or perhaps have a better relationship with your family. Goal-smashing is not complicated, you just need to:

 Define your goal.

 Know your motivation.

 Gather your resources.

● Create and commit to a plan.

If you don't have these things in place, it's like making a cake for no reason with no ingredients and no recipe. Potential disaster.

the science bit

Big goals on their own can make us feel frustrated – we need a lot of small wins along the way.

Scientists have found dopamine levels rise in our brains when we feel satisfied or energised by something we receive or have achieved. Dopamine is also known as a 'feel good' neurotransmitter because it makes us feel happy. You can keep your dopamine levels up by setting small goals and then accomplishing them.

commit to action

Scientists asked people who wanted to reach a certain level of fitness to complete this sentence: 'Next week, I will exercise on [DAY] at [TIME OF DAY] at/in [PLACE].' And literally write it down.

Those completing the sentence were three times more likely to actually exercise compared to a control group who did not make plans.

Committing to action is hugely beneficial.

smart goals

Effective goals are SMART:

Specific, **M**easurable, **A**ttainable, **R**ealistic, and **T**imely.

Here is an example:

I aim to raise £500 for charity by car boot sales in six months' time

OR...

I will learn to play a tune using both hands on the piano using YouTube in three months.

Try and think about your goal in relation to the SMART acronym.

one step back – a goal-setting exercise

You have to see a bullseye before you know where to aim an arrow and in just the same way you need to define your goal before you can make plans to achieve it.

I'd wish you luck with smashing your goal but you don't need it because you have a plan (and that is much more useful).

Draw, write or create a mood board for your goal. Give it lots of detail and think about how it will make you feel to reach it. Really visualise it and bring it to life.

Now take one step back – what's the action you would need to take before you reach your end goal? Write that down then consider what the action before would need to be. Document that too. Keep stepping back until you get to where you are right now.

Now you have a series of small steps that will lead you to your big goal. You know exactly what you have to do.

be happy be you...

...by taking small steps towards your big goal and enjoying each step of the journey.

16 the power of movement

Exercise equals endorphins.
Endorphins make you happy.
Anonymous

We all know exercise is good for our bodies, but it also has a pretty profound effect on the mind too. Runner's high, yoga glow, footballer's pride – exercise is packed with feelings.

Tapping into positive feelings is all about finding the right exercise for you. Don't be afraid to try different things until you find a combination that sticks, and try not to write a sport off completely because of one bad teacher or experience.

the science bit

Young people should do at least 60 minutes of activity every day to stay mentally and physically healthy. Only 14 percent of boys and 8 percent of girls aged 13–15 years are meeting these guidelines. The first thing we'll look at is how to make upping exercise easier on your mind.

Researchers at Arizona University found that when it comes to helping to lift anxiety and depression, exercise seems to work better than relaxation, meditation, stress education and music therapy. It's hard to motivate yourself when you don't feel great or you are busy though, so we have some great tips to help you build a routine.

overcoming barriers to exercise

First choose which activity you're going to do. Maybe you already do some sport, maybe you're not sure, in which case why not think about sports you already enjoy or ask friends what they enjoy.

Plenty of sports can be started immediately from scratch with next to no equipment and can be done from home, with a little bit of help from the internet. Yoga With Adriene is fantastic for beginning yoga, Joe Wicks is legendary for his HITT workouts, and the Couch to 5K is a tried and tested way of getting you from nothing to running five kilometres.

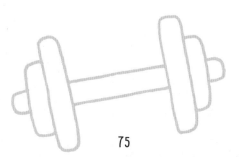

schedule your motivation

Exercise is important, but it doesn't always feel urgent in the same way that tasks that have a deadline – like homework – do. It is so easy to put it off, to say you will go for a run tomorrow, go for a swim at the weekend or try that YouTube yoga class in the morning. Except it never happens!

The urgent-important matrix is a time management exercise that divides tasks up in terms of whether they are urgent or important. Our urgent tasks often end up taking priority over ones that are important but not urgent.

- Important activities have an outcome that leads to us achieving our goals.

- Urgent activities are often the ones we concentrate on because the consequences of not dealing with them are immediate. Sometimes they are about other people's goals more than our own goals.

With exercise, the most important thing ever is not to waste energy worrying when you will do it, schedule it instead.

Put exercise tasks in a diary, calendar, weekly schedule or set digital reminders.

Build a journal page where you colour in a medal, a square or a space each time you exercise.

rituals kickstart routines

Fail to prepare, prepare to fail.

Lay your kit out, text yourself the link to the exercise video, leave out a glass of water, decide on your route. Do everything possible to make it easy to get started.

power cue

Decide on something small that starts your exercise routine. It could be getting a glass of water, rolling out an exercise mat, slowly lacing your trainers. Tell yourself it is this task you are doing, not the whole exercise routine. Eventually this will become a power signal to your brain, and as soon as you do it the rest will follow.

be happy be you...

...by scheduling important, not urgent, tasks and using rituals to get you moving.

17 happy studying

The only place where success comes before work is in the dictionary.

Vidal Sassoon, superstar hairdresser

Okay you may think we are going a bit far to say we can help you be happy about your homework and exams. They probably don't make anyone want to dance in the street or sing. But let's be positive! There are a lot of things you can do to make your homework and revision a happier experience.

the science bit

Exercise first. According to Dr Douglas B. McKeag, exercising before we study can boost our brain power, since even a short workout has our bodies pumping oxygen and nutrients to our brain. This makes us more awake and able to take on new information during post-workout study sessions.

time management

Time is one of the key factors that can make or break a study plan. Try booking slots to study on a visible timetable, just as you would schedule in football practice or a party. Otherwise study just gets crammed into spare moments and is not given the energy and focus it requires.

good planning

The key is to know exactly what is expected of you in your exams and assignments. If you're at all unsure, go back to your teacher and ask. Do use past papers or revision materials that have been written specifically for your exam board – you need to be studying the right information.

If each study session has a planned and specific goal it will give it purpose and be much more effective (as will the sense of achievement/ happiness). Try listing each subject and topic for revision so you can see that it is all going to be covered in your schedule.

having a productive workspace

Working at the edge of a messy kitchen table five minutes before dinner is not ideal. You need a space of your own with your pens, paper and study books next to you and any other equipment you need within reach. A glass of water, good light and a comfortable chair all help too.

Some people work well with background music, some like an open window, and others like the timer on. Tailor your work environment to what works best for you.

neat notes

Neat and readable notes that summarise your learning into clear, simple points are invaluable, and mind mapping can be hugely helpful too. Notes need to be stored in a good system in a specific place.

focus

Do try and minimise distractions – music with words, a mobile phone, a rumbling stomach and a head full of worries will all interfere with studying. Blocking social media during study times will really help. There are apps you can download to block any sites you like for a temporary period.

study partner

Most people do work best on their own, but having a friend or two on hand who might be able to explain indecipherable notes or remind you how to do compound fractions will be really useful. Maybe there's someone in your family who has been through exams before – talking to them about what helped could be useful too.

study skills activity

Three things you can do immediately are:

1 Set up your timetable (a paper one works best) and enter slots for your homework/revision.

2 Identify a workspace and set it up with everything you need.

3 Ensure you have the phone numbers of potential study partners.

Just making a start will make you feel more in control and happier as a result.

be happy be you...

...by implementing these study skills. They are simple, practical and will make your studying more efficient and more time-focused. Keep your eye on the prize and don't forget to exercise!

happy
relationships :)

happiness is entwined with other people

Stick with us on this one. We know it doesn't always feel that way. Siblings break your stuff, parents are on your back, friends seem to be leaving you out, classrooms and corridors full of teenagers make you feel anxious, and teachers give you nothing but stress. Well, yes, other people can be really irritating.

Teenage years are a time of massive change in relationships. You're becoming more independent of your parents or carers and this can be emotional for both sides. They always knew you would grow up but suddenly they're claiming *you turned into a teenager overnight*. You might feel the same, or you might feel like a kid trapped in a teenager's body or a teenager trapped in a kid's body. There might be conflicts as you and your parents try and work it all out.

For many teens, romantic relationships, or a lack of them, become a big thing, along with a confusing bunch of hormones and complex emotions. Your emotions might seem to all happen at once and you are right – research proves it – teenagers' emotions are more complex.

friendships change a huge amount too

Evolving friendships are part of your quest for self-identity and you might find you identify more or less with certain people, and that friendships change more rapidly. Peer pressure comes along and it can be both positive and negative. Negotiating different groups of friends and having a much bigger peer group at secondary school can feel overwhelming at times.

have you ever felt lonely?

It's tempting to retreat to your room, hide under the duvet and play music really loud until everyone goes away.

And that is a great solution sometimes.

But finding happiness on your own can be very lonely, and it can feel like a huge weight and responsibility. A recent study found:

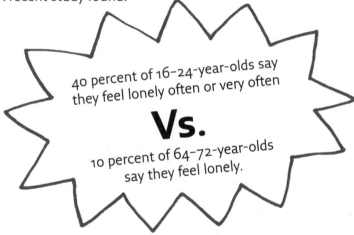

40 percent of 16–24-year-olds say they feel lonely often or very often

Vs.

10 percent of 64–72-year-olds say they feel lonely.

It's one thing to enjoy your own company, and that's great, it is a really important skill. But feeling disconnected from the world like you have no one to talk to, or like no one understands you, is lonely.

are you an introvert or extrovert?

Introverts are people who get more of their energy from solitary pursuits, whereas extroverts get more of their energy from being around other people. It doesn't matter which you are, though, research shows that introverts and extroverts are both happier when they spend some time with other people.

The truth is we need a balance to be happy. We need time alone to reflect, look inside our heads and enjoy a bit of solitude and recharging. We balance this with the need for love, support, encouragement, inspiration and entertainment that other people provide.

However, our world is becoming weighted towards being more solitary in lots of ways. We disappear into our own world via smart phones. Yes, we have friends inside our phones, but researchers found that those who report feeling the loneliest tended to have more 'online only' friends.

Watching the same TV show, at the same time as family or friends, used to be the norm, and gave people similar things to talk about. Nowadays 45 percent of people watch a programme or film alone every day. In the UK, 33 percent of households say they sit together in the same room watching different programmes on different devices.

interconnectedness

People listen to mindfulness apps, do yoga, read self-help books and practice self-care. All of these are really important and powerful happiness tools. But humans really do need to be sociable too!

We have massive potential to spread a little happiness every single day in the simplest of interactions with people we meet. Sharing a smile with a shopkeeper, a compliment with a friend, a thank you with the bus driver, might seem small at the time, but we are all interconnected.

Recent research proposes our social interaction potential across our lifetime is HUGE! On average we live for 78.3 years. Most of us remember people we meet after age 5.

Assume we interact with 3 new people daily in cities, 365 days in a year plus leap year days is 365.24. In total it will be (78.3 – 5) x 3 x 365.24 = 80,000 people.

Over your lifetime you have the power to spread a little extra happiness to 80,000 people.

This section is packed full of tricks, hacks, tips and strategies to help you improve your relationships with other people. It also explores how helping others, being grateful for relationships, and nurturing them can make us all happier.

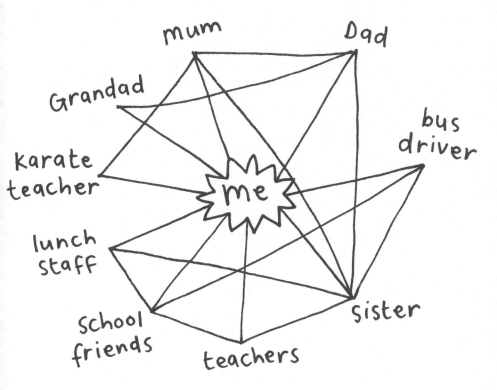

18 fantastic friendships

There is nothing better than a friend, unless it is a friend with chocolate.
Linda Grayson, author

As you go through your teen years your social groups become as (or even more) important than your family. You instinctively turn to your peers to find a place to belong and to explore who you are.

A tribe is a group of friends who share interests and values and who care for and encourage each other. Being in a group of friends where you feel you fit in can bring you a great deal of happiness and security at an often confusing time.

the science bit

Psychologist Abraham Maslow identified the need to belong as one of the five basic human needs, as illustrated below in his Hierarchy of Needs theory. It is natural to want to be part of a group and to feel loved and accepted by others. The need to be part of a peer group is particularly strong in the teenage years as you want more independence from your parents but still want to be part of a supportive unit – but one that's based on equal relationships. It's a practice run for adult life.

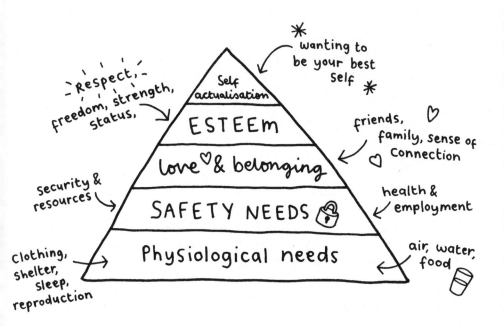

clicks or cliques?

If you click with your tribe you will feel you fit in,
it is as simple as that. You will be able to be you.

But what about cliques? (Small close-knit groups of
people who do not readily allow others to join them.)

You all know who the popular tribe are in your school,
but just because they are the popular ones it doesn't make
them the right tribe for you to aspire to be in. Cliques
aren't necessarily made up of people who share values and
interests and who 'get' each other. They are often groups of
people drawn together because of the perceived power and
popularity associated with belonging to the clique.

But being part of the 'popular crowd' can be hard work.

Many members of these groups lack the self-esteem and
confidence to be their own person, and depend on the
group for their identity. If you don't keep up and fit in you
may soon find you are out.

Not a healthy place to be you at all!

new tribes

The social groups you once enjoyed may well change too
and this is okay and natural. You're not the same person
you were at 11 and neither are your friends. Don't be afraid
to step out of a tribe that behave in a way that doesn't sit
with your values or makes you feel uncomfortable.

Have a think about all the places you might meet a group
of people that you fit in with and feel comfortable with.
This doesn't need to be at school – it could be with your
cousins, a religious community, an LGBTQ group, a sports
group, whatever works for you and makes you happy.

Some groups you belong to will be really meaningful, others perhaps more based on a fun, shared interest.

Gather your courage and take the first step.
You don't need to go again if it's not for you.

appreciate your friends

It is very easy to take people who care for you for granted. But friendships need to be nurtured and valued in a practical not just an emotional sense.

If you think of friendship as a verb it can help you see that you need to take action in regard to appreciating your friends:

- Say thank you when your friend shows up for you.

- Make a fuss of their birthday.

- Check in with them to see how things are.

- Spend time doing fun things with your friends (not just dumping your problems on them).

Basically treat them exactly how you would want them to treat you.

compliments

Giving out genuine praise whenever you can will make your friends feel so good about themselves and will make you a lovely person to be around. To the brain, receiving a compliment is as much a social reward as being given money.

(It has also been shown that people perform better when complimented so, if you need someone to help you, tell them they are doing a great job!)

pom poms and hot chocolate

Just thinking 'Yay! Well done,' is not enough. Sometimes when things are going well for them your friend will need you to show up, give them your energy and encouragement, and cheer them on.

Just thinking 'Oh no, poor you,' is not enough either. When life is tough your friends will need you to show up with support, a blanket, hot choc and a hug.

Basically you need to show up in the good times and the bad and lift your friends up on both occasions.

we are all imperfect

But while good friendships need to be healthy, respectful and a two-way street, they are never going to be perfect. You will fall out, annoy each other, and let each other down occasionally, because this is a relationship and in all relationships that's just how things roll. Your friend (just like you) will sometimes have not-so-great days.

Forgiveness, compassion and acceptance are important in friendships. And on bad days maybe it's time to be an even better friend? Saying 'Hey, you seem unhappy, do you want to talk?' is so much more helpful than moaning about your friend's moodiness behind their back.

what does a good friend look like?

/ Have a think about all the characteristics you would want in a good friend. Go wild with your list and add to it whenever you feel inspired. So, what matters to you? Is it loyalty, fun, homework help, sharing their best playlist, never nicking your boyfriend or girlfriend, lending you their bike?

Once you have your list ... read it again. Can you take on board the qualities you have described and be the kind of friend you would like to have?

be happy be you...

...by being a positive, proactive member of each tribe you are in and making sure to include everyone. Arrange social events, encourage others and do your bit to make the group a really positive place. Your vibe attracts your tribe so send out that positivity!

19 resolving arguments

The volume of your voice does not increase the validity of your argument.
Steve Maraboli, author and speaker

Do you ever feel like you have no self-control whatsoever and that when you are angry it just pours out of you and you say things you really don't mean and it all gets a bit out of hand? Lots of teens feel like this and it isn't just down to hormones (or annoying parents/siblings/teachers/friends). Arguments (especially with parents) are very normal during the teen years.

Part of that is due to the fact that you have a teenage brain.

the science bit

In a test, adults and teenagers were shown a picture of a person's face and had to choose whether the emotion expressed was fear, shock or anger. All the adults correctly identified the look of fear, whereas only about half of teenagers got the right answer.

Interesting...

Researchers have found that in teenagers the prefrontal cortex is still developing, so they rely more on their limbic system. The limbic system is less accurate at identifying other people's emotions than an adult's prefrontal cortex, and is also more emotional, so teenagers are more likely to misread an emotion and overact while doing so.

None of this bodes well for a teenager in an argument...

so what can you do?

Psychologist Marshall Rosenberg, who developed the nonviolent communication approach, found that, if both sides agree to simply repeat what the other side just said before they start speaking themselves, conflict resolution is reached 50 percent faster. Reflecting back the other person's perspective helps to make the other person feel understood, which in turn increases the likelihood of finding resolution.

If things are really heated and emotionally charged, it can also be really helpful to acknowledge the other person's feelings and show empathy. By doing this, 'emotional flooding' is reduced and the other person is able to able to think more calmly and clearly.

If you show someone you have heard how they feel and what they have said they can relax and won't go on and on stressing their point. This is not the same as agreeing with them. For example:

'You sound really angry and I understand it's because you felt Jay wasn't listening.'

'I can hear how frustrated you feel because Archie is often late.'

● Using I statements

Whilst it is important to say how you feel in an argument it is important not to attack the other person. They will only get more defensive. Try using I statements:

'I get upset when you shout' is so much less accusatory than 'You really upset me when you shouted at me', but still makes your point.

If things aren't calming down and the argument is stuck (or escalating) walk away before things get out of hand. This is not weak, it is really smart and gives you both a chance to calm down and find a peaceful resolution in the end.

Research shows that stress-induced changes in our bodies make logical thinking harder and increase aggression. Taking steps to calm ourselves allows us to do the clear thinking and careful listening needed for resolving arguments peacefully.

problem solving

Once you are calm and they are calmer try asking this question:

How are we going to solve this together?

(It shows you want the argument to end and that you are ready to move onto problem solving and that you want to do this together.)

learning from experience

Next time you have an argument put the above into practice – if nothing else try that last question. Write up how it went and what you could have done differently and keep on practising. You'll be working for the diplomatic service in no time at all!

be happy be you...

...by listening to other people's opinions, being calm and clear about what you want, and working together to resolve conflict.

20 building a support network

What do we live for if not to make the world less difficult for each other?
George Eliot, author and poet

It's not a sign of weakness to ask for help, it's a sign of maturity and strength and shows your growing independence.

Being able to turn to people you trust and who you know will help you is vital. Accessing the help you need, not only as a teen but throughout your life, is a key factor in your resilience – your ability to cope when times get tough.

You can find out about the kind of support networks available to you by gathering information from your school support unit, local library, online searches and asking around. You will need to be proactive and gather up your courage to take the first steps but you will find it so beneficial once you do.

the science bit

Family therapist Joelle Johnson has found:

'Clueing others into the problem, the simple act of reaching out to another person to share emotional struggles can be cathartic in and of itself. Feeling cared about, understood and experiencing the compassion and concern from another person can lessen the intensity of feelings.'

It does really help to ask for help.

identifying support

Think about the kind of support you may need during your teens. Once you identify who can help you will begin to see how diverse and wide-ranging your support network can be. Jot down two possible supporters under each area that impacts you. Don't forget your extended family – blood ties and shared history can count for a lot!

Gender and sexuality
Questions you have around gender and sexuality may feel very private and possibly uncomfortable. Where could you go with these questions? Is there a youth group you could access with counsellors or support workers? Do you have a family friend or member you could confide in? Who could help?

1

2

Physical health

How's your health? Are you happy with your fitness levels? This is the only body you will have and taking care of it is vital in leading a healthy life. Could you talk to your parents about healthy eating or find a peer to run with?

 1 _____   2 _____

Emotional health

Who are your best cheerleaders when you need motivation and encouragement? If you are really struggling with anxiety or stress do you feel you could go to the school nurse or counsellor or perhaps you have an aunt who listens well? Where would you turn?

 1 _____   2 _____

Education

What educational support is there for you if you are struggling? Is there a homework club at school you could attend? Is there a trusted teacher you could approach for guidance over revision skills? Do you have a big sister who might help you with your algebra?

1 _____   2 _____

Relationship issues

Whether you have struggles with your family, friendships or a girlfriend or boyfriend, relationship issues can make you despair, particularly if the person you have problems with is usually the person you would get support from. Do you have a relative or a social worker, cousin or other friend you could confide in?

1

2

_____   _____

Identifying, establishing and building up support networks in your life is one of the most powerful things you can ever do for yourself. Getting help when you need it can be both life-changing and life-saving.

how to be a good supporter yourself

Support systems are incredibly important to our wellbeing. They consist of helpful people who can steer you in a good direction. You may be in someone's support system too. Maybe your little brother turns to you for guidance, maybe you are vital to the kid you are teaching to read or perhaps a key part of your granny's care team. If you are, relish your chance to give back and be reliable, kind and giving, or get extra support if you cannot provide it.

be happy be you...

...by having a superstar cheering squad who've got your back.

21 positive peer pressure

> Always remember that you are absolutely unique. Just like everyone else.
>
> Margaret Mead, anthropologist

When it comes to teen life, peer pressure is blamed for lots of things – knife crime, drugs, underage sex and gangs. It's a fact that peer pressure is, to a large degree, a catalyst for lots of risky behaviours.

Peer pressure is when people your own age exert influence on you to behave differently to how you would normally. It is powerful stuff. 55 percent of teens who tried drugs for the first time said they did it because of their friends. 33 percent of teen boys said they felt pressure to have sex before they felt ready because of pressure from their peers.

Generally, people don't want to look stupid, feel left out or laughed at, and they do want to fit in.

the science bit

Peer pressure works because of how our brains work. Neurological studies prove that the medial prefrontal cortex and striatum (areas of your brain that are wired to recognize rewards) both show increased activity when you win amongst your peer group than when you win alone.

We are hard-wired towards the impact of peer pressure. We crave and get a buzz from peer approval.

But is all peer pressure unhealthy? Absolutely not.

positive peer pressure

We tend to think of peer pressure as a negative influence, and of course it can be if it encourages you towards negative or unhealthy behaviours. But some peer pressure can be positive. One study in a hotel placed two different signs above the towel racks urging guests to reuse towels. One sign asked the guests to join the others in reusing towels and the other was a simple request to save the environment. The guests exposed to the peer group sign were 25 percent more likely to reuse their towels.

So, if you need to get studying, then surround yourself with studiers. If you need to get out of a group that's drinking too much or is taking drugs then joining a sports group may be a better option as their focus will be more on healthy living and respecting their bodies.

Peer pressure can lead to very positive changes among groups of people and it is now accepted, from psychology through to advertising, that positive peer pressure is more powerful than just giving people scary facts.

Hanging round with great people with fantastic values is the best way forward.

how to resist

We respect the fact you already know why underage drinking, drugs, knives, gangs, etc, need no place in your life. Schools, your parents and common sense will have taught you this again and again.

BUT

It is sometimes a struggle to resist negative peer pressure and figure out how to say no without possibly losing friends or being considered uncool. This is why even smart people give in.

Have a think about the following scenarios:

Your friend tells you your new glasses are uncool and you should seriously think about getting contact lenses like her.

What could you say?

Your group are all going down to the park to smoke and invite you along.

What could you say?

Your friends are sharing rumours online about your friend and urge you to put them on social media.

What could you say?

One standard response to all the above is to say 'No, I'm not comfortable with that', or 'No, that's not for me', or 'I'm happy as I am.' Using I words means you are not judging your group for what they are doing you are just saying 'No, I'm not doing it because I don't want to'.

If you give an excuse such as 'Sorry I can't today because I'm busy', or 'Oh, I'm not very well', you will just get asked again and again. You have to be clear it's an all-time no.

Now be prepared. Your peers may not respect your decision and may keep pushing or criticise you for saying no.

The truth is that sometimes the only way out is to risk being seen as uncool and losing that group of friends. But if that's the case, focus your mind on what you have gained. Your health, safety, the chance to find a more positive peer group, a clean record, and self-respect...

be happy be you...

...by being unique. Hold onto your own high standards and only be pressured into doing things you know are worth it.

VIB (very important bit): If you are still being pressured to do anything that makes you uncomfortable, seek help from an adult you trust.

22 planning a digital detox

We live today not in the digital, not in the physical, but in the kind of minestrone that our mind makes of the two.

Paola Antonelli, museum curator

Minestrone is a such a great metaphor, don't you reckon? It's a yummy thick Italian soup with loads of different veggies and pasta so it's pretty nutritious, but there is a lot going on in that soup, and just like the internet, it's sometimes hard to work out what is what.

the science bit

Research into social media is as conflicting as you would expect – it is a whole digital world and we all navigate it differently. Social media can lead to FOMO (Fear of Missing Out), it can encourage us to compare ourselves to others, it can make it easier for people to bully others and make misunderstandings more likely. It can disrupt sleep.

On the flip side it can help our mental health by helping us stay connected and to find our tribe. In one study YouTube scored highly for self-expression, awareness, self-identity and community building, but scored low for helping sleep.

Recent research into video games have shown that gamers get a boost from games, seeing improvements to their problem-solving skills, spatial awareness, memory, attention, concentration, IQ, and reading speed. On the other hand, some gamers show signs of brain changes associated with addiction, although research needs to look into whether real life problems have driven some people to play more than is healthy.

why might you need a digital detox?

If you feel like you are checking your phone a lot, answering messages late at night, getting so wrapped up in a video game or YouTube video that you don't want to do other things, or getting irritable when someone asks you to stop, then a digital detox could help.

Having a digital detox every now and again can help you take stock of how healthy your digital life is and remind you what you love about the physical world.

plan a digital detox

Planning your own digital detox makes it easier to stick to and more fun. You could do it one day each week after school, for a whole day or a weekend. Experiment to see what works best for you.

1   Set a date and time for your detox.

2   It might help to let some people know, so you don't have to worry about replying to messages or people thinking you are ignoring them. They might want to join in the detox or help you.

3   Plan fun, distracting, engaging activities offline that you enjoy. The more you can find yourself in the flow with other things, the less you will experience FOMO or the temptation to check your phone. Getting out for the whole day somewhere can work really well.

4   Just before your start time, turn off notifications and delete apps (this is just temporary).

5   You can even put an elastic band or cover (an old sock will do!) over your phone to remind you not to check it.

longer term measures

Lots of devices have ways to set limits on your use.

Removing notifications puts you back in control.

Putting devices out of your bedroom can really make a big difference. Go old school and get an old-fashioned alarm clock or a radio.

 What did you learn about yourself from your digital detox?

Having lived without it this long, is there any device or app you think you can do without permanently?

Were there particular things you really missed or didn't miss at all?

Would you consider setting a regular time to repeat the experience?

be Happy Be You...

...by keeping in control of your internet use and using regular digital detoxes to reflect and reboot.

23 happy healthy relationships

Daring to set boundaries is about having the courage to love ourselves even when we risk disappointing others.

Brené Brown, research professor

Hormones affect emotions and make teenagers more attracted to relationships, but the complex feelings that accompany them can be very overwhelming. And it's not just being in a relationship. Having a crush is stressful too. And let's not forget the struggles of not being in a relationship when everyone else is.

the science bit

Researchers used brain imaging to show that when a person develops a serious crush, twelve areas of the brain work in tandem to release euphoria-inducing chemicals such as dopamine, adrenaline and serotonin. This all sounds amazing in theory, but adrenaline is a stress hormone and dopamine is a feel-good hormone. With all these chemical reactions going off inside your body it's incredibly important to have healthy boundaries in place.

healthy boundaries

Have a look at what relationship experts at Relate class as healthy boundaries for teens:

- When to say 'I love you'. It is okay not to feel that way straight away. Everyone reaches that point at different times.

- Time with friends. You should always feel able to hang out with friends, and people of the same or opposite sex, without having to ask permission.

- Time without each other. You should be able to tell your boyfriend or girlfriend when you want to do things on your own, and not feel like you have to spend all your time together.

- Digital and social boundaries. It is important to talk about whether it is okay to post about your relationship or not, to follow each other's friends or to use each other's devices.

- Physical acceptance. Some people pick up distorted ideas about sex, bodies and relationships from pornography and the media. Body confidence is so important, partners need to respect your body as it is.

- Setting sexual boundaries. You have the right to decide when and if you will have sex and what sex acts you are comfortable with. It is important to talk about this with your boyfriend or girlfriend.

- Consent. Both people must feel safe and be in full agreement about sex acts. Even if you give your consent, it is okay to change your mind at any point.

expressing boundaries

It can be tricky to assert our boundaries and ask other people about theirs if we haven't thought about or practised them. Practise with these sentences:

I am comfortable with....

I am not ready for...

I would like to just...

Let's stick to...

Do you want to...

That's not for me....

I'm happy as we are....

How do you feel about....

Do you feel comfortable if we...

Are you ready to try...

fixing conflicts

Everyone sees things differently, the important thing to decide is if you can compromise. Arguments can be tricky, and often what you are arguing about isn't the real problem.

Try to balance both your needs and work out what is really the problem. Try to stop and think about what the feeling is really about, why you are feeling that way and where it is coming from. Is it about a boundary, a pressure, a feeling, a doubt, a worry?

Talk, and try to stay calm while you explain what is bothering you. Check out the chapter on resolving conflict for tips.

Look for a compromise, but don't compromise on your boundaries.

non-negotiable boundaries

There are some things you should never compromise on:

1. Making you feel disrespected.
2. Not being open and honest.
3. Disregarding what is important to you.
4. Verbal and emotional abuse.
5. Physical violence and abuse.
6. Controlling behaviour.

be happy be you

...by defining your relationship boundaries.

24 talk so parents will listen

> Success is due to our stretching to the challenges of life. Failure comes when we shrink from them.
> John C. Maxwell, leadership expert

A bit like a snake sheds its skin, through your teenage years you will shed some of the skins of childhood. That can scare both you and your parents, but it is a normal part of growing up and becoming more independent.

the science bit

Research shows that teens and their parents see the way teenagers change very differently. In a study of 2,700 German teens, the young people rated their personalities twice, at age 11 and age 14. Their parents also rated them. When it came to 'agreeability', the parents saw a much bigger decline than the teens.

Does this sound familiar? Do your parents or carers think you are more argumentative than you feel you are?

In the past, experts thought that tension and family conflict were necessary during adolescence so that teens could become independent. But new research shows that teens who have more conflict with their parents continue to have struggles and don't do as well in adulthood.

Teenagers see rebellion as marking their individuality from their parents. But parents see it as a challenge to their job of keeping teenagers safe and happy.

In actual fact rather than being about independence, rebellion is an act of dependence.

Rebelling often depends on annoying the person you want more independence from.

Which is why rebellion leads to more stress.

You need to shed your skin and become more independent, you absolutely do, but there may be another way to be different and to gain independence, a way that means less stress for you and fewer arguments from your parents...

Talking sounds obvious, and probably a little painful, but it makes you independent and grown up, without the stress and tension of being rebellious.

It's reverse psychology.

talking so parents will listen

Take one situation that is causing you stress, something you want to be allowed but think your parents won't allow.

What do I need?

 Do I really want this or do I feel pressured into it by others? (If you do feel pressured by friends you might find the tips on peer pressure helpful.)

 How can I show I am grown up enough to handle it?

 How can I convince my parents/carers I will be happy and safe?

 What are their concerns? (Asking them calmly gives you a chance to provide solutions.)

 When is a good time to talk about it? (Sometimes asking for a time to talk about something can be better than blurting it out when they are already stressed.)

when they still say no!

Sometimes parents just can't budge and this can be really frustrating, but doing the following might help:

● Try and listen calmly to the reasons why – feedback is useful.

- Ask what you can do to be allowed what you want.

- Channel your energy into working on proving you can be trusted.

when nothing convinces them...

Wanting to rebel is often a sign you are ready for more challenge in your life, that you are ready to grow up a bit more.

Psychologists suggest the *antidote* to rebellion is challenge.

Is there another challenge you can take on?

It's less embarrassing to tell your friends you can't do something because you are learning to rock climb, playing guitar, cooking sushi, drawing people, making films or chatting to someone who does your dream job.

/ Challenges I want to take on...

Invest your rebellious urges into exploring the grown-up you want to be.

You might want to look at the chapter on goals for inspiration.

be happy be you...

...by reflecting on what independence really means to you and looking for opportunities instead of rebellion and conflict.

25 surviving separation

> There is no such thing as a "broken family." Family is family, and is not determined by marriage certificates, divorce papers, and adoption documents. Families are made in the heart.
>
> C. Joybell C., writer

42 percent of marriages in the UK end in divorce, and 4 in 10 cohabiting couples separate by their tenth anniversary. Whilst that's a huge number, it does not change the fact that this is a massive, often confusing and upsetting thing to experience and it can turn your world upside down.

So how do you survive your parents' separation – when it first happens and later when the dust has settled?

when it first happens

Let yourself grieve. Your parents separating can feel like bereavement, a huge loss of stability and security and of all things familiar. You may feel devastated, hurt, sad, angry and confused. You may feel like this even if your home life had been unhappy and full of arguments. Let yourself feel, name your feelings and talk about them with someone you trust.

do not blame yourself

You are not the cause of your parents' separation. Their relationship is theirs alone – you didn't break it and you can't fix it.

refuse to be your parents' sounding board or go-between

You do not have to listen to the sorrow, anger or accusations one parent may feel towards another, or to any complaints about money, custody or housing that may arise. You have every right to say:

'Please don't involve me in this, talk to someone else about it instead.'

They are adults and landing their worries/complaints on you is unfair. Don't be their go-between either – they need to communicate directly with each other, not through you. Keep your boundaries clear on this.

get some support

Your parents may not be the best people to help you in the midst of divorce or separation as they are probably going through a lot of emotional angst. Finding an understanding person to talk things over with will be invaluable. Perhaps you have friends whose parents have separated, or an understanding aunt or teacher? Do reach out; it's important you have support.

moving forward

As time moves on, separation can still prove tricky so here are some tips from a teen who has been there to help things run much more smoothly:

- Use your phone to keep in touch. Perhaps you could share the TV shows you are watching, or articles you think the other person might be interested in.

- When you are on holiday with one parent, FaceTime the other so you both still feel connected.

- Invite both parents to important events like matches and plays at school – even if it's not your day with them.

- Make future plans with your parents so even if you don't see one for a while you have something to look forward to.

- Find things in common that you enjoy doing with each of your parents. Separation can bring one-to-one time that is really precious.

- Teach your parents about social media, so they can share photos and updates with each other of the things you do. Perhaps create a family WhatsApp group, if their relationship is good enough?

- Have a space that you love at both houses and put effort into making those spaces special.

- Don't feel bad if you have a great time with one parent and think it will make the other sad. Your parents want you to be happy and their feelings are theirs to deal with.

- You could even, further down the line, help your parents with dating profiles (but make sure they're not both using the same websites!)

(With thanks to Felicity Flood for her tips)

control what you can

Now every situation is different and a lot of the above tips will depend on your parents co-operating with each other. Whether they do or not is not something you can control. But you can control a lot of things: the support you get, asserting your right to be neutral, expressing how you feel.

be happy be you...

...by taking care of yourself and giving it time. Most things do turn out okay in the end.

26 *surviving loss*

To live in hearts we leave behind is not to die.
Thomas Campbell, poet

Losing someone you love is probably the saddest thing you can experience. Nothing breaks your heart quite like it and the grief can feel endless and overwhelming.

So why are we talking about loss in a book about happiness?

Grief is complicated, messy and it can last a long time. But you have to go through it to come out the other side. It can feel very much like depression and it can feel absolutely overwhelming to be so sad.

the science bit

George *Bonanno*, who conducts research into grief, has been looking at how we cope with loss and his findings are reassuring.

In his book *The Other Side of Sadness* he says that suffering loss is a normal part of life and that the grieving process is something we all go through. Though it can seem overwhelming, for most people it is an experience that we learn to live with.

In simple terms he's telling us that grief is a natural part of living and we will get through it intact no matter how hard it seems.

Remember, your feelings are entirely normal and you are hardwired to come through it, the same but different.

don't bottle it up

It would very glib to tell you happiness is a choice when you have a broken heart. Of course you are terribly sad and it's very important not to push that (or pretend that) away.

Do lean on those who love you, treat yourself very kindly and let it out. Bottling it up doesn't really work – it will either build up and burst out of you or you will be so full of your feelings of grief that they will leak into everything you do. Neither of these is good for you (or anyone else) so do talk, express your feelings and cry when you need to.

When someone you love dies you will most likely feel a barrage of emotions from anger to denial to guilt, to sadness, to blame and back again. This is entirely, but horribly, normal. One of the worst feelings can be the emptiness, the lack of all the loveliness of having that person you loved in your life.

This you can do something about.

celebrating their life

It is a truth that we only mourn because we have loved.

It can be hard initially to think about all you shared with the person who has gone because of how sad you feel. It is tempting to push away any reminders of them as they hurt so much.

Your emotional bond with the person who has died doesn't die with them. You can still feel connected through memories and through shared experiences. Keeping these alive and in your life helps you focus on the love rather than on your loss. Keeping these alive helps you focus on the life of the person you are missing, rather than on their death.

Becky says, 'My mum loved big, bright, fragrant roses and for a long while after she died when I saw these my heart hurt. Now, a few years later, I fill my house with colourful roses and I think of her and smile as I imagine her in her garden. I am so pleased she introduced me to roses. Keeping them in my home keeps her with me.'

giving thanks

Think about the person you have loved and lost, perhaps you'd like to stick a photo of them in this book.

What wonderful things did they introduce you to, share with you or bring to your life?

Write a little thank you letter alongside your photo acknowledging all of these things and expressing your gratitude.

You don't have to lose these things.

Most of them can most definitely be carried forward into your life. Letting them live on continues that person's impact on your life and helps you celebrate it. It is their gift to you.

Treasuring and cherishing their life means carrying them forward, celebrating and remembering them as you grow, letting them live on through you. To see light you have to look for it.

/ You may want to make a fuller list of all the things that come to mind when you think of the gifts and legacies your loved one gave you. You can keep this in your journal and keep adding to it. This will capture your beautiful memories and is a lovely way to keep them with you going forward.

We are sending you a big, gentle hug.

Dear

be happy be you...

...by celebrating the legacy of those who you have loved and lost by keeping their gifts to you in your life.

27 family tree

You don't develop courage by being happy in your relationships every day. You develop it by surviving difficult times and challenging adversity.

Epicurus, Ancient Greek philosopher

Family trees come in all shapes and sizes and nowadays we understand that the shape of modern families varies hugely.

Knowing more about our family can help to deepen our relationships and our sense of belonging. It can also make us more resilient which in turn can make us happier. The study and tracing of lines of descent is known as genealogy.

If you don't live with your birth family, you may have more than one family tree, and some parts of your family tree may be unknown to you. We've included suggestions for different types of family with the activities in this section.

the science bit

Researchers at the Universities of Graz, Berlin and Munich have discovered that thinking or writing about recent or distant ancestors led students to feel more in control. When they did a test after thinking about their ancestors they attempted more questions and performed better!

The study explains that our ancestors managed to overcome all kinds of problems, like severe illnesses, wars, loss of loved ones, money problems and many more, so when people think about their ancestors it connects them to the powerful knowledge that humans can successfully overcome all kinds of struggles and tough challenges.

Just think of all the things your ancestors must have survived for you to be alive today, you can guarantee someone survived an illness, someone a war and someone a failure or money problem in order for you to be here.

There is so much resilience in every ancestral line.

Genealogy: Where you confuse the dead and irritate the living.
Author unknown

an example of a family tree

Sarah is thirteen and has an eleven-year-old brother called Alex. She wanted to be able to help explain her step and half siblings better to her friend.

She has a mum (Marie) and dad (James) who are divorced. Her dad has remarried, to Kelly, and they have two-year-old Chloe, Sarah's half-sister. Her dad has one sister called Molly, who is adopted and married to Steve, but they have no children. Her dad's parents, her grandparents on this side of the family, Chris and Charlotte, are both alive.

Her mum has a new partner called John. He is separated from Eleanor and they have two children, Lois and Annie, who are Sarah's step sisters.

Sarah's mum has one brother called Peter, who is married to Robert. They have two children, two-year-old Milly and four-year-old Oliver, who are Sarah's cousins. Sarah's grandad (George) on her mum's side died aged eighty. Her grandmother Valerie is still alive and is seventy.

KEY

People

☐ male

◯ female

▽ gay

▽ lesbian

☺ bisexual F

☺ bisexual M

◯ ◻
transgender
M&F F&M

◇ pet

Events

'08─┐ birth
    ☐ year

130

My Family Tree

Children
twins
identical twins
bio-child
adopted
fostered
unknown
pregnancy
miscarriage
abortion
Still birth

b.1940 George 80 — b.1950 Valerie 70

b.1954 Chris 74 — b.1952 Charlotte 68

Rob ▽ Peter ▽ Eleanor John '77 Mum (Marie) 43 '74 Dad (James) 46 '78 Kelly 42 Molly 37 Steve 35

Milly 2 Oliver 4 Lois 15 Annie 21 08 Alex 12 06 Sarah 14 Chloe 2

06 / 14 birth year & age
m.2011 marriage
/ separation
// divorce
immigration
lived in 2+cultures
▲ family secret

131

creating your own family tree

You will need a big piece of paper – wallpaper lining is inexpensive and very long, or you could stick pieces of paper together as you go along. It can be hard to know which direction you will end up going in at first, so use pencil and see it as a rough draft.

1. Start with yourself and work up and out.

2. Talk to family members, ask for their help filling in the bits you don't know.

There are lots of ways to approach a family tree. Every family is different and our reasons for wanting to create the tree in the first place can be very different too.

- You may have more than one family tree – for example birth, adopted, care or foster family.

- You might want to focus on mapping out three generations.

- You might want to fly as far as you can into history along one specific branch of your tree.

- You might want to find a way to map a step or blended family.

- You could use a family tree to better understand a complex family situation.

- You might want to create a piece of art incorporating photos or sketches of people.

- You might want to leave room for a mini biography under each person.

- Sometimes tracing your family tree can be uncomfortable for you or for your family members, so always try and be sensitive and talk it through.

- Symbols can be used in a family tree as shortcuts. There are examples in the family tree on page 131 or you may want to create your own.

other family history projects you might enjoy:

- Recreate-an-ancestor photo challenge.
  Can you recreate a family photo from years ago?

- Create a favourite family recipe or even a book.

- Interview a relative about a time in history.

- Take photos of family heirlooms, ask about their history and use and turn them into a digital booklet.

- Make a film about one person in your family, about a family event or even your everyday life.

be happy be you...

...by creating a family tree, thinking about the resilience of your family or ancestors, and celebrating your family history through a creative project.

28 super siblings

> We came into the world like brother and brother, and now let's go hand in hand, not one before another.
> **William Shakespeare, playwright**

If you are having a hard time with your siblings and there is a lot of conflict it may reassure you to know that over time conflicts usually fade. Not all of you will have siblings so feel free to skip this one if it is not for you, or focus on a cousin or another family friend you are close to.

Whether you are older, younger, the same age, one of two or one of twenty-two, your sibling relationships matter. Why? Because they are probably one of the longest relationships you will ever have and the people you will share a huge amount of your big life events with.

Getting along with siblings can sometimes be really tough though, for two reasons:

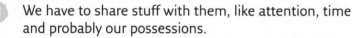

1. We have to share stuff with them, like attention, time and probably our possessions.

2. We do not choose our siblings. So, unlike with friends, if we don't get on we are pretty much stuck with them, at least until one of us leaves home.

Nightmare.

No, not really! Siblings can be your biggest cheerleaders and allies, and they could well end up being your best friend too.

the science bit

Research has discovered that by the time children are 11, they have devoted about 33 percent of their free time to their siblings – more time than they spend with friends, parents, teachers or even by themselves.

Scientists believe that it is our relationships with our siblings that really form us – so it's really important to try and have a good relationship.

7 top ways to get along with your siblings

In all relationships you normally get what you give. Try being a fabulous sibling and just see what happens.

1. Support each other – go to their netball match and help them with their homework, invite them to your show.

2. Do fun things together – like playing board games and baking.

3. Empathise – try and understand how it feels to be older/younger/dumped by their best friend and give them some TLC.

4. Communicate – tell them what's going on in your life and ask what's going on for them. Don't take each other for granted or ignore each other.

5. Find common ground – have a good moan about Grandad's smelly socks or Mum's gnome collection, the things you uniquely share.

6. Respect each other's space – don't read their diary, wear their clothes or use their toothbrush. Respecting their space is respecting them.

7. Appreciate difference – you might have been raised the same way and share you parents, but you are absolutely individual. Appreciate their differences to you and value them, after all it wouldn't be great if you both wanted the last peanut butter cookie would it?

If you are having a hard time with your sibling and there is a lot of conflict, just remember that this often passes.

So just hang in there. In the long run this will probably be one of your happiest and most supportive relationships.

Just a word: sadly, a tiny minority of sibling relationships are toxic and abusive, and hanging in there just isn't the right thing to do. If you are worried that this is the case, talk to a trusted adult for advice.

sharing memories

Get yourself comfy with a pile of family photos and look at all the fun times and experiences you have had with your siblings over the years. This should remind you how important your siblings are and quite how much you share in the way of people and memories. Yours is a relationship to cherish.

You may want to sit with your sibling whilst you do this and relive some precious moments and memories, with them alongside.

be happy be you...

...by valuing your relationship with your siblings and making it as good as it can be.

29 the amazing power of listening

If we were supposed to talk more than we listen, we would have two tongues and one ear.
Mark Twain, author

People often like the sound of their own voice, don't they? Does this conversation pattern sound familiar?

'I bought a white shirt last week it was…'

'Oh, did you? I bought a new shirt yesterday. I saw Joe at the shops he…'

'I saw Joe last month, he said he has a new cat called…'

'Oh my BFF has a ginger cat. He's so cute.'

What a rubbish conversation! No one is able to fully make their point and each person is only interested in getting their own story out.

Do you catch yourself doing this? If you do, then try asking the other person more about their thoughts instead. The rewards are huge for both of you...

 You can learn from other people's stories and perspectives – stepping outside of your own bubble shows you a rich, interesting world.

 Listening to others builds trust and respect in your relationship.

 It can take the heat out of arguments – when you let people know you have heard how they feel, they don't need to tell you again and again!

It makes you a really appealing person to be friends with – people love to be heard and to feel understood.

So if you want deeper relationships, fewer arguments, and a more interesting world then listen up!

Did you know the word listen contains the same letters as the word silent?

One of the most amazing ways to have a great conversation is to hush. But you need to hush attentively. Listening, as opposed to simply hearing, is active not passive.

the science bit

Our listening brain is wired to evaluate and judge what we hear and to solve problems. And that's not in line with active listening at all. Recent thinking in cognitive neuroscience believes these skills developed to help us be more efficient. We have to override this neurological tendency in order to be an active listener, and so we have to be purposeful and focused in our approach.

10 steps to active listening

1 When you find yourself getting distracted, notice and pull your focus back.

2 Don't interrupt, it tells someone you are not interested in them.

3 When you want to interject your opinion let it go. Become curious about their view instead.

4 When something is unclear, avoid misinterpretations or guessing by asking them to clarify.

5 Use visual cues such as nodding and smiling to demonstrate listening.

6 Use nonverbal sounds to indicate you are listening and to prompt.

7 Summarize what you have heard to let the speaker know you understood.

8 Ask open questions like 'How did that feel?' or say,... 'Tell me more' to encourage them to open up.

9 Notice their body language – it is talking to you too and is often louder than words!

 10 Listen only to understand, not to criticise or persuade.

happy listening

A good way to start being a better listener is to engineer situations that encourage people to talk. Over the next week, once a day have a go at starting positive conversations focused entirely on someone else. Your role is simply to be a great listener.

Start by asking questions that make them feel enthusiastic and energized e.g. 'What did you do at the weekend?' or 'Where are you going on holiday?' Really listen to their responses and encourage them to tell you more through prompts and body language.

Actively listening to people's good stories is just as valuable as listening to their sad stories and will make other people feel all kinds of fantastic.

How did it feel to be an active listener? Did it get easier for you? Will you keep this up?

be happy be you...

...by keeping your ears and your heart open.

you and the world

This chapter is all about a relationship which has the power to make you, others and the world much happier. It can help you dive in and explore your place in the world, and fill it with wonder and awe.

When we think of changing the world, it's easy to feel intimidated but we have some brilliant examples of how to do that, and how simple it can be.

We can always do something to make a difference.

And there are plenty of teenagers who have turned very simple actions into change.

You always have more influence than you think. Actions you take, no matter how small, will create ripples of change.

One tiny action can cause a whole chain of events...

ways to change the world

There are lots of ways to change the world and they suit different types of people. Which ones most appeal to you?

- Give time, money or creative ideas to charity.

- Volunteer or team up with others to improve something.

- Monitor the power and influence that governments and organisations (like your school) have. Look at ways to make sure systems are as fair as possible for all groups in society and that everyone has a voice.

- Stand up and protest about an issue that you feel strongly about. Go on a protest march. Write to your MP.

- Change something you do and maybe encourage others to do it too.

- Be a global citizen. Volunteer, experience and learn about the world. Develop new attitudes and ideas to help change.

- Be the person who takes the lead and organises others.

Can you think of any more?

There are so many ways to make the world happier. Here are some activities to help you explore how you can contribute to a better world

30 we can be heroes

I think a hero is any person really intent on making this a better place for all people.
Maya Angelou, author and activist

What makes a hero?

Research suggests that heroes possess some of the following eight traits: smartness, strength, resilience, selflessness, caring, charisma, reliability, and being inspiring.

What do you think?

Heroes must resonate with us emotionally too, which is why different people are inspired by different heroes.

the science bit

We can all be heroes.

Psychologist Frank Farley explains there are two types of heroism. Big H Heroism involves a potentially big risk such as getting hurt, going to jail, or even death. Small h heroism involves things many of us do every day, that don't involve personal risk; helping someone out, being kind, and standing up for justice. We can all make a big difference.

find your hero

Greta Thunberg made a stand about climate change at the age of 15, leading to her speaking at the UN Climate Change Conference and to European leaders.

Jack Munroe has campaigned against hunger and food poverty and created amazing recipes on a shoestring budget on her blog and in cookbooks.

Thirteen-year-old Lily Rice became a Radio 1 Teenage Hero. She is thought to be the first European female to perform a backflip in a wheelchair, and helps other young people to access wheelchair motocross.

Malala Yousafzai was the youngest person to receive the Nobel Peace Prize after writing about the Taliban political movement in Pakistan not letting girls go to school. She was shot by members of the Taliban but survived. So many people protested and signed petitions, that a new bill to change education in Pakistan was introduced.

Spend a little time researching heroes and heroines that inspire you. Who has made a noise about a cause or issue that matters to you, has helped others or changed something for the better?

Find that emotional connection, maybe the cause they support appeals to you, maybe their words move you to act too, maybe you have similar skills or interests?

Collect pictures of your hero (or heroes), quotes, stats and facts.

Make a collage, using your finds.

Display it somewhere it will continue to inspire you.

 What have you done recently that is heroic? What would you like to do next?

be an activist

Lots of heroes are activists, people who campaign for change in the world. Here are some ways to exercise your heroic, activist muscles:

- Sign a petition or create one.

- Write a post on social media or for a school newspaper or write into a magazine.

- Write to your MP – google 'find my MP' to get their name and email, or many MPs are now on social media. But always be polite and factual, even if other people aren't!

- Ask others for help.

- Join a group or charity.

- Wear a badge – get people talking about your cause.

- Join a peaceful protest.

never underestimate your influence

We don't always realise how much we influence other people, but what if just one person takes more action because of something they see you doing? And if they influence one person, and then they influence someone... It soon multiplies and spreads!

It can be easy to feel anxious, overwhelmed and unsure where to start. We can feel powerless when we feel strongly about a cause and read bad news about it. Climate change, for example, can make people feel a number of different emotions, including fear, anger, feelings of powerlessness, or exhaustion.

Doing something will always make you feel better than doing nothing.

Start with a small step. The secret is to recognise you can't change everything, so choose one cause and give it your voice and energy to start with.

Don't try and be a perfectionist, aim for progress instead. So, if you are trying to reduce plastic and end up buying a plastic bottle, don't beat yourself up and just give up!

Don't try and do it all alone either, join a group, surround yourself with like-minded people and get other people to help.

be happy be you...

...by looking for the heroes and heroines that truly inspire you, and being an activist yourself!

31 awe moments

> We're all talking about the same thing, whether it's religious people or New Age spiritual people or Buddhists or scientists. We're all talking about having a sense of awe and wonder at something grander than ourselves.
>
> Michael Shermer, author

Think back to when you were small, what sort of things made your eyes as big as dinner plates, your jaw drop and a great big wow pop out of your mouth? It might just have been a lolly the size of your head, seeing an animal for the first time, a present, meeting a hero or heroine in real life, or perhaps the first time you saw the stars in the sky.

Kids naturally experience 'childlike wonder'. As we grow up we sometimes need to remind ourselves to keep this sense of wonder in our lives, to keep experiencing moments of awe.

If you want to change the world you need to step outside yourself, and challenge yourself to truly believe in even bigger things. Like awe moments...

the science bit

Dacher Keltner is a scientist at the University of California, Berkeley who has spent much of his career understanding the feeling of awe and its effects. He describes awe as 'the feeling we get in the presence of something vast that challenges our understanding of the world.'

Awe is vast and triggers you to feel small, but not in a way that makes you feel unimportant. Awe makes you feel a sense of something much larger than yourself.

It is so hard to explain that feeling of awe, but when you have an awe moment it's like pure childish wonder, free of negative emotions like doubt, fear or jealousy. It feels so good!

When have you been in awe of something?

Awe makes us feel happy, peaceful, energised, excited, inspired, calm. It stops our mind wandering and makes us feel present in the now.

It is so important to fit some awe into your life.

awe-inspiring activities

- On a starry night, wrap up warm, take a blanket outside and stare at the stars. Bring a friend and some hot chocolate for the perfect awesome moment.

- Go outside and look at the sky. Lie down if possible and spend some time looking for shapes in the clouds. J. K. Rowling dreamed up the idea for Harry Potter staring out of a train window, so don't be afraid to daydream, you never know where it might take you.

- Plan a trip to see an amazing view. You don't need to go far, it could be the view of your home town or city from a hill or tall building.

- Visit an art gallery. Try to relax and let your mind draw you to the artworks that inspire awe in you.

- Research, read or watch videos about people who have done awesome things. TED talks are always a fascinating place to start.

- For instant awe watch a video about somewhere amazing. The earth seen from space is always incredible. Or how about these places?

Serengeti, Tanzania

Yosemite National Park, California, USA

Zanzibar, Indian Ocean

Giant's causeway, Ireland

Waitomo Glowworm caves, New Zealand

Fairy Pools, Scotland

Aurora Borealis, Iceland

Arashiyama Dinosaur Provincial Park, Canada

Write about an awe moment you have experienced.

Stanford University researchers found that people who wrote about an awe moment reported stronger feelings of awe, less time pressure, and were more willing to give time to a charity.

Being in awe connects us to the world we live in, it makes us feel smaller and bigger at the same time and gives us a profound sense of wonder at the world. Who knows where it will lead us?

Go forth and be in awe!

No sight is more provocative of awe than is the night sky

Llewelyn Powys, writer

be happy be you...

...by always looking for awe moments and by writing about awesome experiences in your life.

32 valuing and celebrating diversity

Diversity is not about how we differ.
Diversity is about embracing one
another's uniqueness.
Ola Joseph, speaker and writer

what is diversity?

Diversity is about taking into account differences between individuals and groups of people, and placing a positive value on those differences.

It can feel safe to spend time with people who share our location and background, culture, sexual orientation, abilities and maybe even our faith. It can be easier to be with our peers than people of different ages, too.

the science bit

Safe, comfortable and non-challenging means we often miss out on the vibrant, interesting and exciting. It is diversity in life that makes it sparkle and shine. Valuing and celebrating it can be one of our greatest sources of joy.

Researchers have found again and again that diverse groups outperform others – whether this be in solving a murder mystery or buying valuable stocks and shares! This is due to the fact that diversity brings value to any team as it brings with it different viewpoints and refreshing ideas.

Living in an 'echo chamber' where everyone says and agrees with the same thing you do may make you fee good but it does not help you develop or grow.

And actually, aren't we all unique and different? Diversity is the one true thing we all have in common.

becoming a world citizen

> We are far more united and have far more in common with each other than things that divide us.
>
> Jo Cox, MP

If you experience and celebrate diversity in your everyday life, you will have regular exposure to people, cultures, traditions and practices that really open your eyes to a bigger, more colourful world. This will help you become more empathic and understanding, stronger in the face of discrimination and an all-round better world citizen. You will see you have more in common than you thought and that new perspectives aren't scary, they are fascinating. It is fun and eye-opening, and enriching to embrace and celebrate other cultures through food, festivals, clothing, music and literature. But getting to know the individual remains key to valuing diversity.

People are as individual as apples.

the apple project

You will need a bag of apples and an open mind for this activity!

Select one apple from the bag of apples. You might at first think this is a bit odd, after all aren't all apples the same?

(Nope.)

Now have a good look at your apple.

Give it a name.

Spend a few minutes turning it over in your hand, feeling its shape, looking at its colour, noticing any bumps or scars.

Pop it in your pocket and carry it around with you for a few hours getting it out to look at it every now and again.

Do a little research on the country/county your apple is from. Sketch your apple. Write a list of all the things you could do with your apple such as apple bobbling or making juice.

It's so interesting and amazing isn't it, this apple you had thought was like all the other apples?

Now take a bite from your apple, savour all it has to give you. Take the seed from the apple and pop it in a little pot of soil so it can grow into a unique and giving tree.

Say thank you to your apple core as you leave it out for the birds.

How interesting have you found this experience of getting to know your apple, its quirks and characteristics and all the value it brings?

People (like apples) can easily be lumped together. By taking the time to get to know and value the individual you will realise how precious and unique someone is and how much they are to be celebrated.

be happy be you...

...by always getting to know an unfamiliar apple

33 random acts of wildness

Look deep into nature, and then you will understand everything better.
Albert Einstein, theoretical physicist

Nature makes us happier and healthier, both physically and mentally. It reduces blood pressure, helps reduce anxiety, improves focus and clears mental fatigue.

Nature has a huge impact on our wellbeing and in return, we need to look after nature's wellbeing. Nurture your relationship with nature with some small acts of random wildness.

the science bit

The Wildlife Trusts set a yearly '30 Days Wild' challenge in June each year, with the aim of helping people to get more involved with nature. The University of Derby studied the impact of the challenge and the results were fascinating.

The University's research showed that when people took the random acts of wildness challenge there was a significant increase in their health, happiness and connection to nature both during the activity and for months afterwards. They also carried on actively engaging with nature.

You don't need to *know* much about nature to appreciate it though. Research is showing that creative activities in nature can impact wellbeing more than knowledge or scientific activities. Although all are great ways to help nature.

Random acts of wildness are simple activities that throw you into appreciating nature, engaging with it, feeling it and sensing it.

random acts of wildness

Your random act of wildness might take a minute or a few hours depending on how much time you have. But each will change you and, in time, the world too.

1. Smell nature. Rub herbs between your fingers, smell a flower. How does it make you feel? Lavender can bring instant calm and rosemary invigorates our focus.

2. Nature tables aren't just for kids, pick some of your nature finds and display them artistically. Feathers in a jar, pine cones in a basket, driftwood on a windowsill, small animal bones, seed heads in a vase, shells on a shelf...

3. Practise your photography skills. Landscapes and plants are a great place to begin as they don't run away. Share your nature pictures on social media and, who knows, you might influence others to try their own random acts of wildness.

4. Clear up a forgotten space. Get some friends together and clear the litter from a park, beach or urban corner.

5. Save a life. Tired bees appreciate a teaspoon with water and sugar to re-energise them.

6 Go barefoot on the grass. There is nothing like the feeling of tickling your toes on dewy grass in the morning to make you feel alive, and perhaps a little giggly too.

7 Go for a run. Being outside, breathing fresh air, feeling your feet pounding on the ground as your mind stills and your body moves through space is a liberating feeling.

8 Invite a friend to go for a walk. It can give you the space and inspiration to develop your friendship more freely.

9 Make a home or feeder for animals in your garden.

10 You might also want to try spending time in the woods or a park to reduce stress and improve feelings of wellbeing. This is known as forest bathing.

/ Sketch or describe a nature experience or find. Try to use all your senses.

be happy be you...

...by having a daily or weekly random act of wildness.

34 spirituality

You have to grow from the inside out. No one can teach you, no one can make you spiritual. There is no other teacher but your own soul.

Swami Vivekananda, Hindu monk

Spirituality is our search for meaning in life. For belonging, peace, awe, contentment, gratitude, and acceptance.

It is thinking about what motivates us at the deepest level.

Our spirituality often comes from a sense of connection to something bigger than ourselves, which could be art, nature, science, religion, culture or, most likely, a combination of ideas. Exploring our spirituality and that of others can help us find a true and useful place in the world.

Spirituality means different things to different people, but our search for meaning and purpose in life is a universal human experience.

the science bit

Did you know that teenagers actually remodel their brains?

Neuropsychiatrist Daniel Siegel explains how that until you are about 11 or 12 your brain takes in information like a sponge, but then it begins to 'prune' all these ideas and to lay down a substance called myelin, which helps you work three thousand times more efficiently.

Teenage brains even change to lower dopamine, the all-important chemical that make you feel rewarded. Your brain is positively challenging you to seek out new things to trigger that much-needed dopamine. You are working harder than ever!

Teenage years are an incredible time when you shed ideas and rapidly sort through what life means to you.

your spiritual adventure park

Psychiatrist Larry Culliford suggests thinking about your spirituality by creating your own imaginary spiritual adventure park. It could be a theme park or a festival site. A place that is yours, a place to learn and have fun in. You decide what to put in it.

Your thoughts about the meaning of life, your motivation, your spirituality, are yours to create, and you can borrow ideas from wherever you like to help you. Art, science, nature, religion, culture all have great ideas to lend, but your spirituality isn't tied to just one area, you don't have to stick to just one of them.

Spend some time daydreaming, visualizing your own spirituality as a festival, theme park or adventure park...

Take a step outside the everyday for a second, the things you do in ordinary life. Your park is a chance to create something extraordinary. Don't be afraid, take some risks, try not to say no to ideas.

What would you put in it to represent what really matters to you in life now? What would you add that you want to explore more in life?

Run through your senses: sight, sound, smell, taste, touch.

Perhaps there is a huge field full of wild flowers, maybe there are religious buildings? What can you see?

Maybe there is a yoga lesson or football match happening in a glade under the trees, maybe there is a lake for swimming, perhaps there is music playing, people dancing or singing together. What can you hear?

Maybe there is particular food that is meaningful to you? Perhaps food from all your favourite cultures. What can you taste and smell?

Would you have areas themed by places that are important to you? What kind of people would you like to join you in your spiritual world? Who will inspire you? Who can you help? How will you show acceptance and diversity?

What kind of awe moments would you have – a unbroken night sky, giant trees, blue skies, a rainbow, a mountain, a waterfall? What kind of experiences can you have here?

What kind of challenges can you try? Will you try something new, achieve those goals? What do you feel?

Will there be secret happiness projects, random acts of wildness?

Are there stalls with information about ideas or causes you care about? Do areas of your theme park change the world?

Is there space to reflect on the meaning of life? Is their space to be grateful? Is there peace and calm? What does this look like? What would you include to inspire yourself, and other people?

Is technology part of your spiritual world, or not?

/ Write a description of your spirituality as if it is a theme park, world or festival. Or why not sketch a map like you would be given when arriving at a theme park.

be happy be you...

...by remembering your theme park as you go through life. Keep adding to it as you discover those things that truly make you excited about life, that motivate you, excite you and soothe your soul.

35 shopping with a conscience

There is no beauty in the finest cloth if it makes hunger and unhappiness.

Mahatma Gandhi, political and civil rights leader

Buying things that haven't caused others unhappiness can be really hard and uniquely challenging for teenagers. Being on a budget and growing constantly can make fast fashion and fast food attractive.

Products are often cheap for a reason – because they aren't great for the planet, or they have been made in countries where people aren't paid or looked after very well. Modern slavery exists. Some food and its packaging can be bad for the environment and for animals and nature. Peer pressure around stuff you own can be hard to deal with. Status symbols like clothes or possessions can create an affiliation with specific groups.

But little changes can make a big difference, and you have more influence than you think over other people's buying habits. You can make buying decisions with a conscience.

Fast fashion means clothes made quickly and cheaply, to keep up with celebrity and catwalk fashion trends, often passing through wardrobes very quickly too. But fast fashion is taking its toll on the environment, compromising the wellbeing of the people who make it, who work long hours for little pay in factories that can be dangerous.

The Dhaka garment factory collapse in Pakistan led to 1,134 deaths and hundreds of life-changing injuries. Many of the global brands involved in the trade were forced to look at where and how they were getting clothes made. Increased pressure on brands has meant that in some factories, safety measures have been improved, but there are still many that aren't safe, and workers complain that brands are pushing prices lower and lower, meaning people are working for a pittance in what is effectively modern slavery.

the science bit

The toll on the environment of fast fashion is high. It takes around 1,800 gallons of water to make a single pair of jeans. 10,000 items of discarded clothing are being sent to landfill every five minutes, equivalent to £140 million in value every year.

Research has also shown that 'social recycling' – or giving old objects a new lease of life by giving them to others – turns them into happiness. The people giving them away feel happy and the people receiving them feel happy too. It's a huge double win!

how to be a conscious fashion consumer

You can make small changes to your clothes shopping that make a big difference. It can be rewarding too. Knowing how to look after clothes, laser-focused shopping for what you really need, finding the best vintage buys and upcycling are all enviable skills to have.

Here are some ideas:

- Get inspired. Rather than hauls, look for #haulternative social media posts and videos that showcase how to get the most out of your wardrobe without buying anything new. Or ask the question #whomademyclothes?

- Keep it simple. Learn how to put together a capsule wardrobe. You'll need fewer items of clothing because everything works well together and you will spend less time worrying about clothes. Win!

- Plan your shopping. Rather than just going out shopping, look at what is missing in your wardrobe. Think carefully, our best buys are the things we wear time and time again – aim for at least #30wears.

- Be informed. Look at the promises of the brands you love on their websites. It might have one of the following on the label: responsibility, ethical code, our ethics, fashion footprint, environment, sustainability. What are they doing to help? Do they have ethical ranges or recycling schemes? Or are they #Greenwashing?

- Swapping is a brilliant way of recycling, giving old things a new life and of having the fun of new things without buying them new, which uses more of the world's resources. Get together with friends to swap clothes, books, games or accessories.

- Look after your things. Learn how to remove stains and repair clothes. It will save you financially and could mean you can make money back by selling things on when you have outgrown them. Knowing that cold water and soap gets out blood stains and washing-up liquid gets out grease is the kind of knowledge people will always thank you for.

- Buy second hand. Charity shops, car boots, online, or second hand shops can be a brilliant source of unique finds.

- Buy the best quality you can afford. Look for things that will last, plus there is more chance you can sell them on when you have outgrown them.

- Learn to upcycle. Making your own clothes or upcycling old things can be an exciting way to express yourself and could even lead to a career in sustainable fashion.

- Accessorize. Invest in things that you can use to make any outfit stand out that you won't outgrow: watches, chains, jewellery, caps. Search fairtrade accessories, they are often cheaper than you would imagine.

other kinds of conscious shopping

Humans are also starting to think a lot more deeply about food, in terms of workers' and animals' welfare, packaging, transport and our food's impact on the environment. Recent research suggests that consuming less meat and dairy is probably the single biggest way to reduce our impact on planet Earth, reducing not just greenhouse gases, but global acidification, land use and water use.

Reducing our plastic use has never been more important. Ten billion tonnes of plastic end up in the oceans each year, with plastic bottles being the biggest culprit. A million plastic bottles are sold every minute. Look around your bathroom to see what environmentally friendly products you could use – try solid shampoos, a bamboo toothbrush and deodorant in cardboard packaging.

More and more young people are realizing that saying no to drugs is about more than their own safety. Drug trafficking funds other crimes like firearms, modern slavery, people trafficking and terrorism. The 'county lines' system of transporting drugs using vulnerable young people has helped to drive fatal stabbings to the highest levels since records began.

be happy be you...

...by using your conscience when you're shopping. Making changes to your consumption step by step can be easier than getting overwhelmed by trying to do everything.

36 experience wish list

Fill your life with experiences, not things. Have stories to tell, not stuff to show.

Unknown

Have you seen your bedroom floor lately?

How much time do you spend sorting out your stuff to give or throw away?

Do you have more stuff than you need?

When you find yourself with some money or feel like you need a treat, do you spend it on experiences or do you spend it on stuff?

Too much stuff can have a negative impact on our mental health and wellbeing.

the science bit

Researchers have investigated whether objects or experiences bring us more happiness, and experiences come out on top each time.

New experiences let us adapt, learn something new about ourselves and develop new ways of thinking. Time spent learning new things, enjoying the company of friends or exploring new places makes happy memories. The happiness we get from objects fades much faster.

One way we can all change the world is to consume less and a great way to achieve that is to experience more.

Experiences can help you find your purpose too. Researchers found that the four common factors in young people who had a strong sense of purpose were:

  travel

  spending time in nature

  volunteering on a project to create social change

reflective practices like journalling, meditation and yoga.

According to psychologist Rich Walker, who analyzed 500 diaries covering 30,000 memories of events, those who engage in a greater variety of experiences tend to be better at holding on to positive emotions and minimizing negative feelings.

Does the idea of joining that football team/street dance class/choir still feel too daunting?

Experiences can feel more scary and unpredictable than buying objects, but do not fear, research suggests that although mastering a new skill may cause temporary increases in stress levels, this stress is outweighed by long-term boosts to positive emotions.

Sometimes you have to try a few things to find your passions and purpose in life.

your experience wish list

Some people make a bucket list, things they want to do before they 'kick the bucket', aka die. But we are all about being happy, so we prefer to focus on the positive!

Create an experience wish list.

Ask friends and family for ideas for your wish list of experiences. Research experiences to try, fun to have with friends, places to go, travel destinations, skills to learn.

Think: what, where, who, why, when?

Zip lining, canoeing, running, climbing a hill, learning to play poker, learning the piano, helping an animal, visiting an art gallery, having a picnic, baking a cake, growing a chilli plant, cooking a curry, photographing a wild animal, riding a rollercoaster, kite surfing, running a race, learning to sing, giving a speech, learning to code, sailing, learning to make clothes, learning to weld, camping, making something from wood, painting a room...

You could write down as many things as possible, or come up with something for each month of the year.

You could create a collage of images to represent the things you want to try. Visualization is an extremely powerful way of making things you love happen!

If you still like buying 'things', researchers suggest investing in items that engage your senses to provide experiences, like books, music, podcasts and even video games. Research shows that listening to upbeat music can have lasting mood-boosting effects too.

be happy be you...

...by choosing experiences over things.

37 inclusion

Inclusion is recognising our universal 'oneness' and interdependence. Inclusion is recognizing that we are 'one' even though we are not the same.
Shafik Asante, writer and African American community leader

Where we are at with inclusion

Over the past hundred years there have been many changes for the better in society in regards to inclusion and civil rights. Sadly, the good bits described below are still only true in some places, and certainly not all.

Women now have rights to vote and work, to control their own bodies, to marry other women and to be paid fair wages. But not everywhere and not always. Women are still wolf-whistled in the street, lose out on promotions due to childbirth and are under-represented in many areas that matter such as policy making.

Race discrimination is now illegal and yet black people continue to be stereotyped, under- represented in advertising and throughout media, and in senior positions in the workplace. Racial abuse still occurs and the colour of your skin can still negatively impact how you are treated.

Disability discrimination became policy long after gender and racial policy changes, and still has a long way to go. Disabled people are still taught separately, denied physical access to buildings and excluded from groups they might like to belong to due to 'access/support' issues that remain unaddressed. Jokes are still made about disabled people and broadcast on mainstream TV.

Gay people can marry in many places now and their rights not to experience homophobic bullying are enshrined in law. History continues to write them out of the picture, harassment and abuse still occur and many gay people are reluctant to acknowledge their sexuality because of fear of being excluded from family or social groups.

Everywhere you look there are examples of people being excluded due to prejudice, discrimination and ignorance.

The world is turning towards greater inclusion and huge strides have been made, but it is slow progress and for those being excluded still, it is an isolating experience.

the science bit

In his book, *A Different Drum: Community Making and Peace*, Scott Peck describes how unhealthy groups can create a sense of purpose and value for themselves by choosing an individual to be their common enemy – you can see this throughout history on a worldwide scale and in schools on a more local level.

The danger is that excluded people then internalize the message that they are 'worthless,' and this can lead to isolation, self-harm and depression.

Imagine not being able to go to school with your peers, being stared at because of your clothes, having to say no to a party because you can't get into the building, have no one talk to you or hang out with you at break, being called names because of how clever you are or how you look.

Being excluded is one of the saddest things that happens in our society and it is totally in our power to change it.

This is a call to action.

There is so much you can do.

own your privilege

Try to understand that you have many privileges, perhaps of health, of wealth, of situation, that may possibly make life easier for you. Many of these things are yours simply by luck. Not everyone has the same opportunities, and acknowledging that is the first step to helping effect change.

be inclusive

Inclusion is both an action and a state of mind. Here are some ideas as starters:

INCLUSION

1. Say hi to the new kids at school, the ones no one has really bothered with.

2. Talk to your youth group about installing a wheelchair ramp.

3. March for gay rights and attend a Pride event.

4. Learn some sign language.

5. Ensure you stand in an arc when you are with a group of friends not a closed circle, this way everyone can be welcomed in.

6. Be curious about other cultures and ask questions, do some research don't make assumptions.

7. Be open to friendships with all sorts of people, this will enrich your life tremendously and help you get along well in a diverse world.

/ What else could you do? Think about people and communities you know and write yourself an inclusion action plan with five things you can do, then act on them.

Then make another list and do them. They may feel like baby steps but they matter enormously. Steps like these break down barriers.

Inclusion has a long way to go but a journey of a thousand miles begins with a single step.

be happy be you...

...by keeping inclusion in your heart and putting it into action every chance you get.

38 no more muddy footprints

It is the greatest of all mistakes to do nothing because you can do only a little. Do what you can.

Sydney Smith, writer and preacher

I bet when you were little you were often told off for stomping muddy footprints around the house after playing outside. These muddy footprints didn't matter much (despite the telling off) as they were soon cleaned up.

No matter what age we are though, we all still leave footprints wherever we go. But the ones we leave on our world now are an entirely different kind. We have to tread much more carefully and considerately if we want to keep our world a happy one – our carbon footprint is not so easy to clean up.

the science bit

A carbon footprint is the amount of carbon dioxide (CO_2) emitted by a person over a period of time. The more carbon dioxide we release into the atmosphere, the worse it is for the environment.

Each and every time you use energy that comes from fossil fuels (such as petrol or electricity from non-renewable sources like coal and gas), you create CO_2 and make your carbon footprint bigger.

Human activity means that the levels of CO_2 in the atmosphere at the moment are higher than they have been at any time in the last 400,000 years, and that's causing too much heat to get trapped in our atmosphere. Global warming – which is sometimes also called climate change – is now starting to cause a significant amount of damage to our planet, and will become increasingly harmful to human health and food and water supplies.

According to the Energy Saving Trust, homes account for 30 percent of the CO_2 produced each year, so less CO_2 from households will make a big difference to our overall carbon footprint.

Being 'carbon neutral' is the ultimate goal towards preventing climate change. Being carbon neutral is basically where your carbon output is reduced to zero.

It's a challenge we have to take on!

a cleaner footprint

Okay we know you don't pay the bills in your house or make the big decisions so we aren't going to suggest you go out and personally get solar panels. Nor are we going to suggest you go and sell the family car on eBay and present your parents with a tandem instead.

However, we do have a checklist of activities for you to try. Tick the square as you give them a go and see your carbon footprint shrink as you do.

Most of your carbon footprint will come from transport, housing and food so these are the areas we are going to address.

You really can make a difference.

be happy be you...

...by taking care of the planet in any way you can.

Could you walk or cycle at least one day a week?

Take a quick shower instead of a bath

Turn off the tap whilst you brush your teeth

Have a look online for recipes to use up any leftover food

Put on socks or another jumper before cranking up the heating

Have a zero spend day on a weekend and only use what you already have

Boil only the amount of water you need in the kettle

Plant a tree (an apple seed will do). One tree can absorb one ton of CO_2 over its lifetime

Drink tap water instead of bottled water. Carry your drinking water in a reusable bottle.

See those clothes on your bedroom floor? Double-check them, I bet they don't all need washing

Go and turn off all the lights in the house that don't need to be on (and have a chat with the bill payers about switching to LED bulbs, which use way less energy)

Unplug every device you aren't using – any electronic gadget you can turn on with a remote uses power even when it is off

Use a laptop, not a desktop computer, if you have a choice. Laptops take less energy (up to 80 percent) to charge and run

Research all the recycling options in your local area

Go through your wardrobe and take unloved clothes to the local charity shop

Offer to hang out the washing to avoid the dryer being used

Have a vegetarian or vegan day

Have a paper-free day (no printing!)

Research local climate change projects or conservation projects online and get involved

Have a family chat about plastic – how can you reduce the amount you use?

Help to write a family meal plan for the week to avoid food waste

Go to the library and take out a book on climate change.

Say no to single-use plastic like straws and cutlery

Try and keep your school lunches wrapper free

Recycle everything you can, all day

Grow some of your own fruit or vegetables

Wrap a gift in fabric instead of paper

39 the secret happiness project

Real generosity is doing something nice for someone who will never find out.
Frank A. Clark, writer

On a really gloomy day doesn't an unexpected rainbow just lift everyone's spirits? A glorious little hit of happiness that resets us and reminds us that the world is full of amazing things.

Have you heard of guerrilla gardeners? They sneak out and plants seeds and flowers in areas that are neglected, unused or overgrown. Street artists create their art on buildings in public places, often in secret and without permission.

It is absolutely time for secret happiness projects to sweep the nation too.

Some of these activities will include giving little gifts, some will involve creating simple works of beauty and some will be thought-provoking or show appreciation. They are all designed for others to just stumble across. These little tiny, random injections of happiness, with you as their creator, will make people smile and may well inspire them.

the science bit

Scientists have found that putting happiness out into the world will make you happier too. When you are generous your brain lights up as if you yourself have been given something nice! You also get a boost of endorphins (just as if you had run a race).

These make you feel fantastic. You feel less stressed and more connected to others too and as a result you will want to give even more. Even the intention of being generous makes you feel happier.

It's powerful stuff.

create your own secret happiness project

1. Write your favourite joke on a postcard and leave it on a café table for the next customer to find.

2. Write happy words or draw happy symbols on stones and leave them dotted around your neighbourhood.

3. Create a little bookmark and pop it inside a library book as your return it.

4. Grab a few friends and spend half an hour litter-picking your local park so it looks its best. No one will know why it looks so much better but they will see that it does.

5. Leave a book you have loved on a park bench with a message on the inside asking the receiver to do the same when they have finished with it.

6. Leave a little bunch of flowers tied to a park bench with a note saying simply, 'For You'.

7. Create a nature window for someone to find – you need four sticks to make your frame and then you make a picture inside with random fallen bits of nature.

8. Got an old cuddly toy? Make him a little sign saying, 'Looking for a new home' and leave him on a wall to be found.

9. Make muffins for your grandparents or neighbours.

10. Chalk a rainbow or an inspirational quote on the pavement outside.

11. Declutter your stuff and drop it at the charity shop. Inside the bag put a thank you card and a packet of biscuits dedicated to the volunteers who work there – sign it, 'From an admirer'.

12. Scoop up all the unwanted clothing in your home from every family member and take it to your local homeless shelter or charity shop.

13. Arrange tiny pebbles into a heart shape and leave them on a park bench.

14. Give out three lovely compliments.

15. Smile at three strangers.

Which one was your favourite?

be happy be you...

...by bringing your secret happiness project to life.

40 nurturing

In spite of unseasonable wind, snow and unexpected weather of all sorts – a gardener still plants. And tends what they have planted ... believing that spring will come.

Mary Anne Radmacher, writer and artist

Have you ever taken care of something and helped it to grow? Perhaps a puppy or maybe some cress? If you have you will know you have to feed it, tend to it and give it all the right conditions it needs to develop.

You have to nurture it.

It may be hard work and it may take a while but oh, when you see the thing that you have invested in flourish, it is so worth it isn't it?

the science bit

Do you that know gardening is considered by some scientists to be a cure for depression? There is actually a specific soil bacterium, Mycobacterium Vac, that triggers the release of serotonin in our brain, so just by getting our hands dirty, we are getting happier.

But there is more...

Dopamine is triggered by the expectation of a reward and, when we nurture something like a seed, we have that expectation and that optimism that what we are nurturing will bloom. Nurturing something to help it flourish creates expectation and makes us feel good.

You might be nurturing your unconfident little sister. You might be nurturing a litter-picking project, or an interest in engineering, or an injured bird you found. You might be nurturing your body after you have been ill or you might be nurturing your talent at singing.

Lots of things need our nurture, our care, our time and attention in order to bloom or to heal. It is the very best direction of our energy.

the plant prompt

Take a little flower seed, any seed will do, and plant it in a little soil. Dedicate yourself to giving this little seed what it needs: light, nutrients, a bit of a chat, a bigger pot as it grows, and replanting when required.

Each and every time you give your seed a little bit of care, consciously remind yourself you are nurturing it in order to help it bloom. Then, each time you do something nice for your seed, do something nice for yourself too: self-hug, play your favourite song, run a bubble bath or text a friend. Maybe you could dance barefoot, watch a TV show you love, write a letter or hug your mum. Let your seed care be a prompt to take care of yourself.

You and that seed will both grow from being nurtured and we want that nurturing to become a habit. Try and see this as a metaphor for your life. In life when you give yourself to others or to the world you always have to fill yourself back up or you will be running on empty and that never works.

Oh, and if that seed falters, gets a bit straggly or doesn't make it, just go ahead and plant another one. We can start over again with good intentions every single day.

Self-care is not selfish. It is self-care and it's very, very important.

And happiness? Well, it's simple really. It consists of lots and lots of little bits of nurture directed towards yourself, other people and the big wide world.

Take care of you x

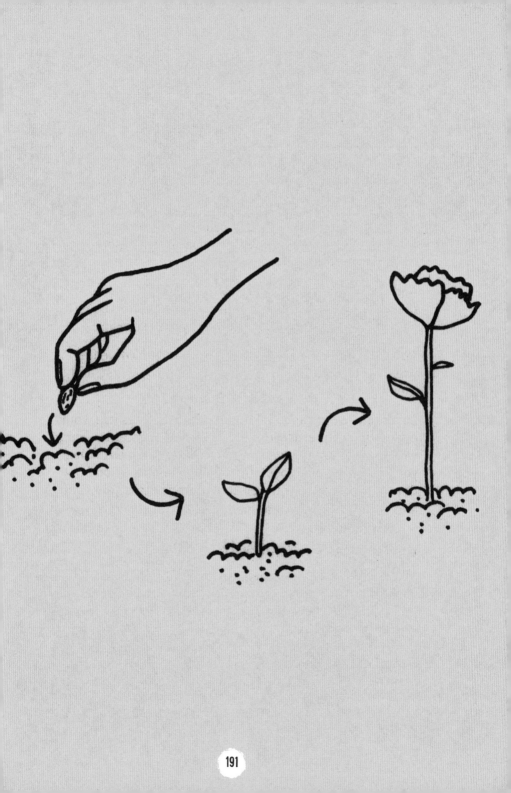

A JOURNEY back to you

Throughout this book we have looked at how you can nurture yourself through taking care of your body and your mind, your emotions and your passions.

We have also looked at how you can nurture your relationships with other people through being a good listener, resolving conflicts, valuing difference and being kind.

And then we have looked at how you can take care of the world through reducing your carbon footprint, being inclusive and taking action for things you believe in.

As we said right at the beginning, you have to come first, you have to nurture you – every aspect of you – first, and then the rest will flow.

Be as kind, caring and loving towards yourself as you would ever be to anyone else, more so if you like – because (yep, we will say it again) you have to come first. And then once you are full, all that good nurturing will bubble up and out of you – because as you well know, happiness is contagious and really cannot be contained.

a promise to yourself

From here on in and throughout your entire life you must vow to be your own wonderful nurturer, your own best caretaker and your own awesome cheerleader.

It is over to you.

Your wellbeing, your happiness, is in your very capable and nurturing hands.

Go forth, be happy, be you!